THE HAGGADAH

A NEW EDITION
WITH ENGLISH TRANSLATION,
INTRODUCTION, AND NOTES
BY
CECIL ROTH
WITH DRAWINGS
BY
DONIA NACHSHEN

LONDON
THE SONCINO PRESS

1934–5694

Printed in England

INTRODUCTION

I

THE SEDER

The Seder Service for the Night of Passover is probably the oldest, as it is certainly the most fascinating, of all rituals of the sort at present current among mankind. Its origins date back for perhaps thirty-five centuries. The most ancient portions of the text are at least two thousand five hundred years old. By the beginning of the Christian era, at the very latest, the text had already received much of its present form; and the latest additions (with the exception of one or two of the hymns in local usage) were completed nearly a thousand years ago. It has had the most profound influence, not only upon Judaism, but even more, perhaps (through the Eucharist service to which it gave rise), upon the daughter religion — Christianity. No human ritual is more assured of perpetuation, and none can be more deserving of study.

The ritual is generally known by the name of *Seder*, or 'Order'. The full title should be 'The Order (of service) for the Night of Passover', or something similar. But so far has this ritual overshadowed all others of the sort in Jewish usage that it is universally known, without qualification, as 'The Seder'. It consists of a number of curious ceremonies of extreme antiquity, based upon the actual usage in the Temple at Jerusalem when the Paschal lamb was consumed, and grouped about the statutory Passover meal. It is thus, in its way, a fossilized domestic feast of twenty centuries ago, with all its distinctive formalities, from the hors-d'œuvre to the dessert. This is accompanied by a running commentary, of prayer and legend and exposition. It is this that is known as the *Haggadah*.

THE HAGGADAH

The whole service is based upon one single Biblical injunction in connection with the observance of the Passover: 'And thou shalt tell thy son in that day, saying, It is because of that which the Lord did for me when I came forth out of Egypt' (Ex. XIII. 8). 'Tell', in Hebrew, is *Hagged*: and *Haggadah* means 'telling'. This ancient ritual is therefore simply the statutory recounting of the story of the Exodus to the assembled household at the time of the Passover celebration, in literal obedience to the Biblical precept.

Originally, this formality took place at the time of the eating of the Paschal lamb on the first night of Passover (the fifteenth of Nisan). Outside Palestine, however, it was impossible, before the fixed calendar was instituted, to ascertain the precise day on which the feasts would be celebrated in Jerusalem. It became customary, therefore, to duplicate the observance, continuing the celebration of each feast over the following day. Thus coincidence with the Palestinian usage, on the one occasion or the other, was ensured. This still remains the custom of the Jewish people, notwithstanding altered circumstances, throughout the Diaspora. Accordingly, the *Seder* is now generally observed in the same form, with inconsiderable differences, upon the two first nights of Passover in succession.

THE COMPOSITION

Something in the nature of the Seder Service has, without doubt, been observed continuously ever since the institution of the Passover itself. In the earliest times, while the Paschal

offering was being consumed with its unleavened cakes and bitter herbs, a simple explanation of the reason for the observance must have accompanied it. To this there would probably have been added a hymn of thanksgiving. Later, a few stereotyped formulæ came to be included: the earliest, perhaps, the Aramaic invitation to all who were hungry to come and partake of the feast. With the period of the Second Temple the ceremonial became a little more elaborate. The words of Holy Writ began to be scrutinized with greater minuteness; further implications were discovered in certain turns of phrasing; more implicit obedience came to be desired. From this period, probably, dates the main outline of the ritual: the Psalms, taken over from the Temple service; the Four Questions asked by the youngest present; and, in answer to these, the formal *Haggadah*, or explanation of the curious ceremonial. The destruction of the Temple in the year 70 led to the cessation of sacrifice and the replacement of the altar by the home as the centre of the proceedings. The Seder Service now reached its modern form down almost to its least detail; and the ritual followed at the time of the compilation of the code known as the *Mishnah*, in the second century, is to all intents and purposes identical with that in use to-day. Since that period a few hymns have been added, a few phrases altered; but no essential modification has taken place. If an English Jew of to-day could be miraculously transplanted to the Palestine or Mesopotamia of eighteen centuries ago, he would find the service (save in one or two unimportant details) perfectly familiar. It is a remarkable and, perhaps, unequalled record.

DIVISIONS

The *Haggadah* proper falls naturally into two main divisions, grouped about the statutory meal which is the *raison d'être* of the whole. The first part comprises the majority of the ceremonies associated with the occasion. The recital is mainly historical and expository, referring to the deliverance from Egypt, and explaining the cause of the celebration. This is the oldest portion of the *Haggadah*, having reached virtually its present form by the time of the destruction of the Temple. It consists to a very large extent of 'Midrashic' interpretations, in full Rabbinic style, of certain Biblical passages relating to the Exodus: some familiar from other sources, others found only here. It may thus be considered an integral part of the Hebrew literature of the Talmudic period.

The distinctive portion, after the preliminary recital of the usual festival *Kiddush*, or 'Sanctification', over wine, is made up as follows:

(i) Display of the Unleavened Bread, serving as the occasion for the asking of the Four Questions by the youngest present.

(ii) The Answer, accompanied by illustrations of the duty to recount the story of the Exodus, and a description of four types of son.

(iii) Exposition of Joshua xxiv. 2—4.

(iv) Exposition of Deuteronomy xxvi. 5—8, leading up to an elaboration of the marvels of the Ten Plagues, and a hymn of gratitude.

(v) Psalms of thanksgiving *(Hallel)*.

(vi) The prelude to the meal, with its attendant ceremonies.

After the meal, and the saying of the ordinary grace, the atmosphere changes. The recital is no longer historical. It is rather hymnal, glorificatory. References to the hopes of deliv-

erance, of the great Passover of the future, become more and more pointed. The door is opened, and a goblet filled with wine, in readiness for the coming of the prophet Elijah, who is to announce the Redeemer. The second part of the *Hallel* and the jubilant Psalm cxxxvi, instinct with hope, are chanted. The *Nishmath* prayer, one of the finest post-Biblical liturgical compositions, is recited, and the thanksgiving closes with a benediction pronounced over a last cup of wine. The ritual concludes with a simple, but deeply impressive, prayer of three words, that the next year may witness the celebration in Jerusalem.

APPENDICES

Originally the service ended here, as it does still in certain rites. But the Jew was never niggardly in his expression of thankfulness, and it early became customary for further hymns to be chanted. Originally, no doubt, the selection was free; but when the *Haggadah* came to be written, as a separate book, and still more when it came to be printed, it inevitably became more settled. The first choice was a staid hymn of the ordinary synagogal type taken from the liturgy of the Passover season. But the Seder Service was essentially one for children (a note, this, which is struck from the very beginning). Their feelings and their tastes were consulted above all at this stage, when, after so distinctively liturgical an interlude, a special effort was perhaps needed to keep them awake. Accordingly, two rollicking mediæval religious folk-songs are chanted, succeeded by a typical 'madrigal of numbers', and finally by an unabashed nursery rhyme barely susceptible of a theological interpretation. It is a somewhat surprising, and certainly unprecedented, finale; but there can be no doubt that Judaism has profited immensely by placing the children first, even in its religious observances.

SOURCES

The *Haggadah*, as a literary composition, is a curious medley. It contains much that is noble, a little that is bizarre, and some elements that are, in the very finest sense of the word, childish. There are represented in it the pure Hebrew of the Bible, the Aramaic adopted during the Exile, the vigorous but inelegant dialect of the Talmudic period, the literary tongue as it was revived in the liturgy, the hybrid used in the mediæval hymnology, and even, in many places, the vernacular — Spanish, Arabic, French, German, or Provençal. There are inserted in it some of the finest passages from the Book of Psalms, associated with this festival from time immemorial, and perhaps in part composed for it. Some portions are taken from the ordinary prayer-book: the *Kiddush*, *Nishmath*, and others. There are quotations from almost the whole range of the Talmudic literature: from the *Mishnah* (second century), which forms its groundwork; from the *Gemara* of Palestine (the so-called Jerusalem Talmud, of the third century) and the fuller and more famous Talmud of Babylon (fifth century); from the *Midrash* and the kindred writings, replete with legend; from the mediæval synagogal hymnology and table-songs. Of the original elements, for which no other source is known, some (like the story of the famous *Seder* at Bene-Berak) are of considerable historical or literary value. The main section of the *Haggadah* is a typical example of the Midrashic literature in its simplest form: a detailed exposition of a Scriptural passage, with all of its implications brought out and supported by the authority of kindred verses. The *Haggadah* is thus an anthology of Jewish literature in almost every one of its multifarious aspects, composed in many ages and under many skies, and moulded by long centuries of usage into an harmonious whole.

CEREMONIES

The *Seder* is not a religious service, in the strict sense of the term. It is a festal meal, accompanied by a running commentary of a religious nature. The meal itself is a very special one. It perpetuates the form of the Paschal supper as it was eaten in the Temple at Jerusalem. It includes, therefore, a number of distinctive ceremonies, each with its own history, going back for thousands of years. These will now be dealt with one by one.

THE UNLEAVENED BREAD

The characteristic feature of the Passover (especially after the destruction of the Temple, when the Paschal lamb was no longer offered) is the Unleavened Bread (Hebrew, *Mazzah:* plural, *Mazzoth*). It is from this, in fact, that the feast receives its Hebrew name, the Feast of Unleavened Bread (*Pesah*, or Passover, is strictly applied only to the first night). The reason is given plainly in the Scripture: how, fearing lest worse still might befall them, the Egyptians hurried the children of Israel away by night, so that they had to snatch up the bread which they were baking before it was leavened. At the same time, on account of its hardness and unpalatability, the *Mazzah* was regarded as 'bread of affliction', serving as a reminder of the harshness of Egyptian bondage. In the Orient, moreover, bread made without leaven was a less expensive preparation, which it took a shorter time to prepare (one finds it repeatedly mentioned in the Bible as being given to a surprise visitor). Hence it remained the poor man's fare. It was, therefore, considered a 'bread of poverty' — fitting token of the slavery which it commemorated.

At a later period a symbolical value was attached to the *Mazzah*. Leaven was regarded as typifying the 'leaven of sinfulness', the evil impulse in man's heart which turns him aside from higher intent. Hence unleavened bread became a token of purity, of the higher freedom which comes from obedience to the better self: 'heavenly bread', as it is called in Jewish mystical literature.

MANUFACTURE

Originally, the *Mazzah* was made at home by the women of the household. This became increasingly difficult, and in the Middle Ages most communities had their own *Mazzah* bakeries, some of which still survive. These at last yielded in turn to specialized manufactories. The corn out of which the flour is made is watched over from the moment it is cut, to avoid any fermentation, however slight. In order to render the cake slightly more brittle and palatable (an object which has been amply realized) it was criss-crossed with lines made by wooden or metal combs or wheels. In Talmudic times, artistic shapes and figures were introduced, but the practice was subsequently given up. In the course of the last century a machine for the baking of *Mazzoth* was introduced, in the face of some opposition, and at the same time the traditional round shape began to give way to square. Still, even at the present day, there are many places in which the *Mazzah* is made by hand in the congregational bakery according to the time-honoured system. The fire for the baking was generally started with the willow-branches used in the previous year during the processions on the Feast of Tabernacles. In the Orient it is customary to keep a single *Mazzah* hanging up in the synagogue throughout the year, so that, in literal obedience to the Biblical precept (DEUT. XVI. 3), a man should remember the coming forth

from Egypt all the days of his life. *Mazzah* may, of course, be eaten throughout the year; but it is customary to refrain from it during the month before Passover, so that the taste of it should be fresh and the novelty unspoiled.

THE SEARCHING-OUT OF THE LEAVEN

The Biblical precept instituting the Feast of Unleavened Bread specifically enjoins that, for this occasion, 'ye shall put away leaven out of your houses' (Ex. XII. 14, 19). The Jew took this and the companion injunctions very literally. Every corner, however remote and difficult of access, was thoroughly cleaned before the Passover. The kitchen was scoured out. Pots and pans were exchanged for others which had not come into contact with leaven. Spring cleaning acquired, in a word, a religious significance: so much so that the Jews may, perhaps, claim the credit of having introduced that hygienic practice. But in spite of all these preliminaries, the statutory 'search for leaven' — now become little more than a formality — remains the duty of the master of the household. It is carried out on the night preceding the Passover (excepting when the first day of the festival falls on Sunday, when it is performed on the Thursday night). Equipped with a feather and a wooden receptacle, which can be burned after contact with the prohibited elements, the head of the family makes the tour of his house by candlelight, searching for any traces of leaven. The housewife has, however, generally done her work so well that the task is superfluous, and it is necessary to deposit here and there a few crumbs in order that the formality may be duly observed. After the search, a declaration is made in Aramaic (the vernacular language of the Jews at the time of its composition) to the effect that any leaven which has not been found shall be considered null and void. Enough bread is left, of course, for breakfast on the following day; the remains of this are burned betimes by the housewife, who accompanies the act with the recital of a similar formula.

THE THREE CAKES

For the Seder Service it is necessary to have three *Mazzoth* wrapped up separately and placed on top of one another on a tray. This forms the centre of the ceremonial: for on these nights it is a duty to eat unleavened bread, while during the rest of the festival it is sufficient to abstain from leaven. It is customary, therefore, for these to be prepared with especial care. Formerly, the master of the household would go in person to superintend the baking of these at least. In England, packets of specially prepared *Mazzoth* for use for the *Seder*, a trifle thicker than the ordinary variety, may be purchased. They are generally known as *Mitzvoth*, as being used for the fulfilment of the *Mitzvah*, or religious obligation: or else, more accurately, as *Shimurim* ('watched').

The necessity for three cakes is not difficult to explain. On any Sabbath or festival it is customary to have on the table two loaves of bread, in recollection of the double share of manna which fell in the wilderness on the sixth day (Ex. XVI. 22). But, as will be seen, one of the *Mazzoth* used during the *Seder* is broken into two at the beginning of the service, half being put away for later consumption. Hence, in order to have two whole ones for distribution immediately before the meal, it is obviously necessary to start with three.

THEIR USE

Of these, in reminiscence of the order in which it is customary to summon persons to the reading of the Law in the Synagogue, the uppermost is called the 'Cohen', the second the 'Levite', and the third the 'Israelite'. The use made of them is as follows:

(i) The 'Cohen' is broken at the beginning of the meal, when pieces of it and of the 'Levite' are distributed to all the company, in order that they may fulfil the duty of eating unleavened bread.

(ii) The 'Levite' is broken towards the beginning of the service. Half is put away as *Aphikoman*, to be eaten at the close of the meal; the other half is distributed with the 'Cohen', as mentioned above.

(iii) The 'Israelite' is distributed, along with the bitter herb, immediately after the first breaking of bread, 'in remembrance of the Temple, according to the custom of Hillel'.

APHIKOMAN

The name and the function of the *Aphikoman*, referred to just above, forms one of the puzzles of the Seder Service. The reason for breaking the *Mazzah* and putting part on one side is none too difficult to understand. According to an old custom in vogue while the Temple yet stood, it was usual to end the meal with the Paschal lamb, so that its taste should remain predominant in the mouth. Moreover, it is likely enough that a portion both of this and of the unleavened bread would be put on one side, to ensure that something should be left over in case of the belated arrival of some unexpected guest. The place of this is now taken by the reserved half of the middle *Mazzah*, which is distributed and eaten at the close of the meal. The word *Aphikoman* is thus derived in all probability from the Greek ἐπικωμοι, or dessert, given a more Hebraic ending by assimilation to a word of similar derivation used in a different significance, at another stage in the *Haggadah*, in connection with the reply given to the Wise Son. The concealment of the *Aphikoman* brings to the forefront the children, whose part in the *Haggadah* is notable. It is expected that this strange procedure will stimulate their curiosity and lead them to ask, spontaneously, the questions which come shortly after in the ritual. The ancient Rabbinical authorities (T. B. PESAHIM 109*a*) had indeed prescribed that one should 'seize' (i.e. anticipate) the *Mazzah* on Passover Eve for the sake of the children, lest they should fall asleep. Accordingly, with pardonable regard for the stricter interpretation, the children are permitted literally to 'seize' the *Aphikoman*, unbeknown, from its resting place, exacting a ransom for revealing its whereabouts when it is required. The *Aphikoman* has an importance of its own in Jewish folk-lore. It was said to prolong life, leading to the expression 'he ate much *Aphikoman*', applied to a person who died at an especially ripe old age. It was customary to preserve a piece of it in the house for luck from year to year. The *Haggadah* itself was the natural place of storage: and little is more pathetic than to discover the little hoards of dried-up *Mazzah* in old volumes, perhaps unused for a century past. In eastern countries it was often carried about the person, to guard against the Evil Eye.

THE BONE

On the right-hand side of the tray is placed a portion of the shankbone of a lamb, roasted. This is intended to commemorate the actual Paschal lamb which was sacrificed in the Temple at the Passover: originally the essential feature of the observance, but now no more than a symbolical relic.

THE EGG

Another of the objects customarily placed upon the *Seder* tray (opposite the shank-bone, to the left) is a baked egg. Many explanations have been given of this. It stands, we are

viii

told, for the free-will festival offering, which accompanied the sacrifice of the Paschal lamb in the Temple; but the connection is not quite clear. Classical scholars, recollecting the description of a Roman meal, 'ab ovo usque ad mala', consider that it is no more than a relic of the customary hors-d'œuvre of the traditional meal of classical times. Others suggest that it is in token of grief for the destruction of the Temple: for among the Jews, as among most Oriental peoples, the Egg — a symbol of resurrection — is the usual mourning fare, which those bereaved are given on their return from a funeral. It is locally customary even to-day, indeed, to begin the *Seder* meal with hard-boiled eggs dipped in salt water. Those who hold this view point out, very ingeniously, that the first day of Passover always falls upon the same day of the week as the fast of the Ninth of Ab, the double anniversary of the destruction of the Temple, which is therefore imagined to be all the more keenly remembered on this occasion. Moreover, according to tradition, the Patriarch Abraham died on Passover Eve. But in point of fact, the Egg is generally associated with this season of the year in popular lore throughout the world; and it may well be that this is merely the relic of an ancient custom, which has been given here a fresh symbolic value. Folk-lore has it that the person who is so lucky as to secure the roast egg of the *Seder* on the second day of Passover, when its immediate use is finished, will be assured of good fortune, and that any wish which he expresses while eating it will be fulfilled.

THE BITTER HERB AND HAROSETH

Besides these objects, the tray contains some Bitter Herb — a reminder of the bitterness of Egyptian slavery — and a toothsome mixture known as *Haroseth*, which serves to modify the sharpness of the Herb. This composition is a luscious medley of apple, almonds, raisins, and cinnamon, all chopped very fine, and made into a paste by the addition of a little wine. Its admixture with the Bitter Herb, modifying its sharpness, may be taken as symbolical of the Divine lovingkindness which qualified the bitterness of the Egyptian bondage. The colour and general composition remind us of the mortar which the Hebrew slaves had to use in the buildings which they constructed for their task-masters. The principal ingredient, the apple, has a delightful legendary connotation. It recalls the ancient account, according to which, after Pharaoh's heartless sentence against their male children, the Hebrew mothers went out to give birth to their babies in the secrecy of the orchards, far removed from human gaze: and there, we are told, angels came down from heaven to succour them. Authority for this delightful fable was found in the Song of Songs: 'I raised thee up under the apple tree: there thy mother brought thee forth'. And the apples in the *Haroseth* remind us of this legendary orchard setting.

THE FOUR CUPS

One of the distinctive features of the Seder Service is the drinking of four cups of wine. Even a pauper supported from the public charity, we are informed, should not have less than this quantity. Not that this is by any means a token of immoderation — the last charge, perhaps, which can be truthfully levelled against the Jew. It must be remembered that these customs had their origin in the Orient many centuries ago, when wine was as common and as necessary a beverage as tea is to-day. The injunction to have four cups of wine was no more than a guarantee of an ample meal; and on this night above all, wine, the symbol of rejoicing, was absolutely requisite. But it is by no means necessary to drain each cup to the dregs, and it is quite permissible to use unfermented wine. However, it must be *kasher*;

prepared, that is, under Jewish supervision, and free from any conceivable suspicion of the admixture of leaven.

That four cups should be prescribed is only natural. The first is used for the recital of the *Kiddush*, or Sanctification, as on every Sabbath or festival eve. The second is the cup of rejoicing, over which the first half of the *Hallel* is repeated, and the 'blessing of redemption' recited. The drinking of the third is in compliance with a common, though not obligatory, Jewish usage in connection with the recital of grace. The final cup is used for the completion of the *Hallel* and the subsequent prayers of thanksgiving (the 'Blessing of Song'). During the course of the meal, wine may be partaken of without ceremony. Afterwards, if required, an intermediate cup may be drunk before the recital of the 'Great *Hallel*' (Psalm cxxxvi), but no more. Four cups, however, are regarded as essential, for the poor man as well as for the rich: a symbol (according to later explanations) of the four synonyms for redemption used by Scripture (Ex. vi) in connection with the Exodus: or of the four mentions of Pharaoh's Cup in the dream interpreted by Joseph (GEN. XL. 11—13): or of the Four Monarchies which are to precede the final Redemption: or of the four figurative Cups of Punishment which the empire of ungodliness is to drain before that event, while four Cups of Comfort are administered to Israel.

SANCTIFICATION

This *Kiddush*, or Sanctification, mentioned above, is, strictly speaking, the formal act whereby the sanctity of the Sabbath or festival is proclaimed. 'Remember the Sabbath Day to keep it holy' (Ex. xx. 8), says the Scriptural injunction: and the Rabbis glossed it, 'Remember it — over wine'. For the Jewish holy-day was essentially a festive occasion, to be celebrated by the enjoyment of the good things that God has lavished upon His world: and where was it more fitting to proclaim its intimate sanctity than over the table, likened in Rabbinic fancy to the altar? The presence of wine on the table was of course taken for granted: and there was Biblical precedent ('Wine... maketh glad the heart of man, and bread... strengtheneth man's heart', Ps. civ. 15,) for giving it precedence over the second staff of life. If this applied to ordinary occasions, how much more so did it to the Sabbath and festivals, when gladness was an essential element in the observance! The 'sanctification' of the day over wine is accordingly a tremendously old usage, dating back well beyond the beginning of the Christian era. In the course of time it became customary in most communities to recite the formula also in the synagogue, at the close of the evening service: apparently for the sake of the wayfarers who were housed there or near by. On the Passover Eve, however, it is presumed that every individual is spending his *Seder* properly, whether in his own home or at that of some kindly fellow-Jew: and the formality in the synagogue is accordingly omitted. In the isolated ritual of the Jews of the Yemen, in southern Arabia, a long and flowery addition is made to the Passover *Kiddush*, in the middle of the main benediction.

When the Festival coincides with the Sabbath eve, the two forms of the *Kiddush*, for Sabbath and festival, are combined. Thus, apart from minor verbal alterations, the description of the First Sabbath (GEN. I. 31—II. 3) is prefixed. On Saturday evening, on the other hand, account must be taken of the *Habdalah*, or 'Differentiation', by which the Sabbath is in the ordinary course of events ushered out. The adaptation for the festival is a prayer of rare beauty and dignity. This is preceded by the benediction of Him who creates fire. According to an old and quaint Talmudic legend, Adam, the Father of all flesh, remained

illuminated by the primeval light wherewith the world had been brought into being until the close of the day succeeding his creation — the first Sabbath. Then he sinned, and it departed. With the fall of night, the world was for the first time plunged into darkness. Man was terrified at the blackness around him, until he had the inspiration of taking two stones and rubbing them together, creating artificial light for the first time. Overjoyed, he blessed the 'Creator of the Light of the Fire'. It is this same benediction which the Jew, prohibited from kindling fire for the duration of the Sabbath, repeats immediately after its conclusion over a naked flame. On an ordinary Sabbath night, a special many-wicked candle serves for this purpose. On a festival, this is unnecessary; but it is customary to set down the wine-glass and to stretch out the hands towards the candles on the table, observing the play of light and shadow, while the benediction is being recited.

COVERING THE MAZZOTH

An interesting example of Jewish idealism finds its way into the *Seder* ritual. The traditional Hebrew regard for animals is well known. Thus, on the authority of a well-known Biblical verse (DEUT. XI. 15), it was prohibited for a man to sit down to a meal until he had fed his domestic creatures. Similar instances, from the Scriptures and from later literature, can be multiplied. This same regard was extended to the inanimate. Thus, on those occasions when two scrolls of the Law are taken out of the Ark in the same service, it is customary when they are put back to give precedence to the one which was taken out first — out of regard, in a manner, for its feelings. The same charming idea finds expression in the Seder Service. During the recital it is customary to keep the *Mazzoth* uncovered, as being the centre of the whole celebration. At certain points, however, the goblet of wine is raised in token of thanksgiving. At these stages it is customary for the *Mazzoth* to be momentarily covered, so that, as it were, they should not witness the slight placed upon them!

RECLINING

In ancient Palestine, the labourer or slave ate his meals hurriedly, squatting down upon the ground as best he could. The well-to-do householder, on the other hand, shared in this respect the habits of his Greek or Roman contemporary. Especially when there was a feast, he reclined on cushions by the side of the table. On this night, at least, there is no such thing as master and man (it is customary, indeed, for Jewish servants to sit at the table with the family). All Israel are equal, all Israel are free men, and all Israel should recline at the table as free men do. True, the ancient customs have changed. The 'triclinium' no longer exists, and fresh class distinctions other than reclining at meal-time mark the difference between rich and poor. Nevertheless, upon the *Seder* Night, the Jew still recalls conditions in Palestine ten, twenty, thirty centuries ago. There may no longer be room for him to recline at full length. But the Celebrant at least is propped up on cushions, on his left side, and the goblets of wine must be quaffed 'reclining leftwards', according to the immemorial custom of the East.

THE SARGENES

It was usual in the old days, and is still among the most traditional, for the head of the household, as he conducted the service, to wear his *sargenes*, or *kittel* — that white, shroud-like vestment associated with all occasions of especial solemnity. He would don it each year as he prepared to receive the Divine judgment on the Day of Atonement; he had

worn it when he stood beneath the marriage canopy with his bride; he would be arrayed in it when he went to his last rest with his fathers in the House of Life. Thus, it was indicated from every point of view as suitable for wearing upon the *Seder* Night. It was a token of purity, it was a token of gladness, it was a token of freedom; and, above all, it was a mystical token of the final deliverance from human bondage and from human misery which that night might be expected to bring.

'The Night of Watching'

'It is a night of watching unto the Lord for bringing them out of the land of Egypt: this same night is a night of watching unto the Lord for all the children of Israel throughout all their generations' (Ex. xii. 42). Thus the Scripture summed up the story of the Exodus. The Rabbis interpreted the text very literally, as was their wont. In *all* generations, they said, this anniversary marked the deliverance of their ancestors from the dangers which menaced them. By a microscopical examination of the Biblical text they found authority for suggesting that a whole succession of miraculous deliverances mentioned in the Bible, from the time of Laban to that of Sennacherib, occurred upon the Passover — a conception embodied in two of the hymns recited at the close of the service. Naturally, the great final deliverance of the future was similarly to take place upon this night, which is a true *Lel Shimurim*, or Night of Watching, unto the Lord for *all* generations. On such an anniversary the Divine protection was peculiarly near to the chosen people. It was formerly customary in some places to leave all the doors unlocked on this night — a courageous action, in those times — as a token of trust in a higher protection. Thus, if the Redeemer came, as he was confidently expected to do from year to year, he would find all ready to receive him. Similarly, the usual night-prayer, in which the Divine protection is solicited, was superfluous. Accordingly, it was customary to repeat, instead of the usual lengthy formula, only the first paragraph of the *Shema* (Deut. vi. 4—9). Is it not possible to see in this, too, the desire to make the evening all the more memorable for the children, worn out by the long and elaborate ritual? The astute Rabbinical explanation, perhaps, comes merely to justify a predetermined conclusion.

The Song of Songs

When the last hymn was chanted, the table cleared and the children dispatched to bed, the older members of the family were not finished. For the pious there was yet another sacred task to perform. In past generations the multiplication of prayers was considered a privilege, not a burden; and men sought eagerly for something else to recite. The choice was an obvious one. From time immemorial, the Song of Songs had been associated with the Passover. Its references to the reawakening of nature had, perhaps, been responsible in the first instance for its association with the Spring festival. But this was not all. The inclusion in the Scriptural canon of this most delicate of love idylls had been justified, among Jews as among Christians, by the reading into it of something beyond its literal significance. Assuredly, the passion that it so exquisitely commemorated was not the carnal attraction of two human beings, but the affection which bound God to His people. The final triumph of true love which it depicts indicated therefore — it was obvious — the ultimate redemption of long-suffering Israel. Interpreted thus, what reading could be more fitted for the Passover season? Accordingly, by the last flickers of the dying festival lamp, the senior members of the family would soar together above the oppressive atmosphere of earthly

xii

cares and strivings into closer communion with the Soul's Beloved: 'Let him kiss me with the kisses of his mouth, for thy love is better than wine....' With these transcendent cadences the ritual of the night would at last close.

Local Usages

The local usages which have grouped themselves round the *Seder* are myriad in number and of fascinating interest. In the Caucasus, the recital of the *Haggadah* becomes an incident of something very much like an old morality play. Several families decked out in their finest gather together in patriarchal fashion to celebrate the feast. As they are chanting their prayers there is a tapping at the door. It is one of the youths disguised as a poor wayfarer from Jerusalem, with dusty shoes and with clothes hanging in tatters from his back, who demands to be allowed to celebrate the Passover with them. After a little parley he is admitted, and besieged with inquiries as to the welfare of the Holy City. He replies by informing the company that they may look forward to the future with confidence. All will be well: for the sages of the Holy Land have instructed him to bring the good news that the Deliverance will not be long delayed.

In the Yemen (*Arabia Infelix*, for its miserable Jewish inhabitants) the *Seder* Service forms a pendant to the baking of the *Mazzoth*, and special psalms and hymns unknown to any other rite are recited. Curiously enough — contrary to the universal tradition of Israel — it is here essentially an observance for the adults, children being actually excluded. It is possible that this is a development due to centuries of persecution. This is certainly the case with the Marranos of Portugal, among whom the recollection of the Passover has survived in a somewhat modified form, but with unabated force. The observance is there postponed to a day later than the correct calendar date — a displacement originally occasioned by the desire to outwit the spies of the Inquisition, who were especially vigilant at this season. The essential part of the ceremony here lies to an even greater extent in the baking of the *Mazzoth*; and the flaring caused by the fragment of dough when it is thrown into the fire (a substitute for the offering originally given to the priest, Num. xv. 17—21) is regarded as a token of good fortune. In the Near East, it is customary to add a number of legendary comments on the *Haggadah*, in Spanish or in Arabic, bearing upon the miracles which took place at the time of the Exodus. In pre-Expulsion Spain, it was usual to read the marvellous tales in connection with that event contained in the fabulous *Sefer ha-Jashar* — the Book of the Righteous. And, on their sanctuary on Mount Gerizim, the exiguous remnant of the Samaritans still carry out the Paschal sacrifice, year by year, according to all the Biblical rites and ceremonies, just as their fathers did a score of centuries ago.

III

The Seder in History

The importance of the Passover as a landmark in Jewish history is not confined to the single occasion of the Exodus. In the Bible itself we read of various notable celebrations: of that 'in the second year after they were come out of the land of Egypt' (Num. ix), when the original precepts were repeated and elaborated; of that celebrated under the leadership of Joshua, on the morrow of the entry into the Promised Land (Josh. v. 10); of the great revivals under Hezekiah (II Chron. xxx) and Josiah (II Kings xxiii. 21—3). In the fifth century before the Christian era, according to recently discovered papyri,

Darius king of Persia issued detailed instructions for the observance of the Passover by the military colony established in Upper Egypt — such was the importance of the feast in that period also. Both Josephus and the Talmud recount, with some differences, how one year, in the period of the Roman domination, a census of the Paschal lambs slaughtered was taken, in order to convince the Emperor that the Jews were no contemptible tribe. According to the lowest figure given, the total came to a quarter of a million; and it must be remembered that at least one whole household was represented by each lamb. It is well known that the vast concourse which had gone up to Jerusalem from all parts to celebrate the Passover, in spite of the dangers of war, was responsible for the enormous numbers to be found in Jerusalem at the time of the last siege. It was a period of the year when, throughout the time of the Roman rule, there were constant fears of a tumult. Guards were maintained in the galleries surrounding the Temple, and the slightest suspicion of disorder was ruthlessly put down in blood. There was long remembered one dark occasion when the Roman procurator, Pontius Pilate (whose name, possibly, has been confused with that of the tetrarch Archelaus), mingled the blood of many Galilean pilgrims with that of their own sacrifices (LUKE XIII. 1).

The loss of the Jewish national centre did not by any means mark the end of the special significance of the festival in Jewish history. It became, however, more and more sombre in its associations. In the age of persecution it was precisely with the Passover that maltreatment reached its climax, year after year. It was the springtide, when human feelings and human passions began to surge more wildly. Armies moved again after the immobilization of the winter. The Christian world was forcibly reminded from every pulpit of its traditional enmity towards Judaism. Now, too, despite the decrees of rulers spiritual and temporal, from the Pope and Emperor downwards, despite the unanimous opinion of scholarship, despite the prescriptions of their law and the dictates of common sense, the despised people were suspected of the darkest of all crimes — that of using Christian blood in the manufacture of the unleavened bread, or for other purposes connected with the feast. The accusation was the pretext rather than the reason; and, from the twelfth century downwards, it served as the starting-point of a long succession of massacres which darkened the joys of the festival. There have been innumerable occasions — in mediæval Germany, in the Spain of the Inquisition, and in modern Russia — when the *Seder* celebration was disturbed by the incursion of an armed mob, and when all who participated in it were dragged off to death on some trumped-up charge, or on none at all. The bitter tragedies of Troyes (1288), of Prague (1389), of Lisbon (1506), and of Kishinev (1903) are only a very few typical examples of that terrible series of Passover massacres, in which myriads of Jews must have met their deaths. In the whole of English and of Jewish history there are few stories more tragic than that of the Great Sabbath on the eve of Passover in the year 1190, when the whole of the community of York, shut up by a bloodthirsty mob in the Castle, resolved to anticipate massacre by suicide, and perished almost to a man. But the eternal message of hope, revived in the Jewish breast all the more ardently by the festival of freedom, saved the martyred people from despair even in this darkest hour.

THE SEDER IN FICTION

The place that the *Seder* has occupied in fiction is notable, though, perhaps, hardly commensurate with its actual importance in Jewish life and with its inherent dramatic qualities. Heine, in German, in his immortal fragment, *Der Rabbi von Bacharach*, easily leads the

way. But he is only one of many writers, including Israel Zangwill in English in *Elijah's Goblet* and *Had Gadya*, and Eça de Queiroz in Portuguese in his inimitable *A Reliquia*, who have succeeded in capturing and reproducing something of the spirit of the celebration at various stages of Jewish history.

IV

THE UTENSILS

For this great occasion of the Jewish year no expense, and no trouble, was considered excessive. The silver lamp or candelabrum reserved for the Sabbath would shed its radiance over a table covered with a snow-white cloth of finest damask. The factories of Faenza, at the period of their greatest glory, turned out dishes for the *Seder* adorned with the customary symbols — the Lamb, the *Mazzah*, and the bitter herbs. The pewterers' craft, as practised in London or Amsterdam in the eighteenth century, is hardly anywhere better represented than in the *Seder* plates, appropriately chased, which they produced in comparative profusion. Wealthier persons used silver, and had the beaker and ewer for washing the hands made of the same precious metal. Richly embroidered cloths, over the making of which the Jewish matrons would have spent the leisure of many long winter nights, were employed to cover the dish. The German Jews invented an ingenious, if not over-elegant, three-tiered dish for accommodating the *Mazzoth*, with a curtain at the side, by drawing which they could be revealed to view at the appropriate moment. But greatest of all was the affectionate care lavished upon the ritual itself.

THE HAGGADAH AS A BOOK

The peculiar position of the *Haggadah* in the Jewish liturgy early led to its receiving special treatment. Its comparative unfamiliarity, coupled with the fact that it had to be used simultaneously by a number of persons sitting sedately around a table, made it advisable for it to be copied and treated as a separate work, though it continued to be included also in fuller compilations. The earliest separate manuscripts extant belong to the thirteenth century, but there can be no doubt that the practice goes back far beyond that period. The festive character of the occasion and the small size of the work itself made it both natural and convenient for extraordinary care to be lavished on it, in the matter both of writing and of illumination.

ILLUMINATIONS

In this latter respect, practice was naturally influenced by environment. In the normal course of events the Jewish artist was trammelled to a certain extent by an over-meticulous regard for the literal interpretation of the Second Commandment, which led him to avoid any representation of the human body. This objection was, indeed, by no means general or absolute until comparatively recent times, when oppression had fostered obscurantism; and some mediæval illuminations are extant which amaze one by their boldness and freedom. Nevertheless, the prejudice undoubtedly existed, and there can be no question that it impeded the development of Jewish art. There were one or two occasions, however, when such qualms could be over-ridden. The *Haggadah*, for the eve of Passover, occupied a special position. It was not, in the strict sense of the word, liturgical. It was not even brought into the synagogue. It was bound up with an occasion of unusual festivity. Its

appeal was specially directed to the women and children of the household, to whom an indulgent eye was always turned. Moreover, its subject positively called for artistic treatment. Hence (with the scroll of Esther, read upon the feast of *Purim*, and — locally — the contracts of marriage) it always formed an exception to the rule dictated by the traditional anti-artistic prejudices, no matter how strongly held. Any person who could afford it had his *Haggadah* illuminated by the ablest artist money could employ; and some of the specimens extant are among the very finest examples of mediæval Jewish art. The pages were engrossed in gold and colours, with grotesques abundantly strewn about the margin. A whole page might sometimes be devoted to one or two words of especial significance. Differences of treatment might indeed be discerned between one country and another. *Haggadoth* of the Spanish school would concentrate upon the Bible story, beginning sometimes with the Creation and expatiating on the events of the Exodus. In these, co-ordination between the text and the illustrations (which might sometimes be included at the close, by way of appendix) was sometimes slight. In Germany, with an artistic tradition somewhat freer, and less trammelled by Moslem anti-æsthetic prejudices, the ritual itself would claim the lion's share. Illustrations would be devoted especially to the preparations for the Passover, the celebration of the *Seder*, and the Redemption from Egypt. The element of humour was not lacking: witness one MS. in which the celebrant is depicted as pointing at his wife when he speaks of the Bitter Herb! If no Jewish artist was available, there was no hesitation in having recourse to a Christian — as, in one famous instance, to Bonifazio il Giovane. Amongst the most noteworthy examples of the work in its illuminated form may be mentioned the Sarajevo *Haggadah*, a Spanish production of the fourteenth century, about which a whole book has been written; the Crawford *Haggadah*, now in the John Rylands Library at Manchester; and the *Haggadah* of Darmstadt, which has recently had the honour of being reproduced in complete facsimile.

Invention of Printing

With the invention of printing, the tradition of the manuscript *Haggadah* was not broken. For centuries after, down almost to the present day, it remained customary for such as could afford it to have the work engrossed on vellum in the old style, at needless expense and not always with satisfactory results. But the competition of the printing-press soon began to make itself felt. In the first edition of the liturgy, published in 1485 by Joshua Solomon of Soncino — the Gutenberg of Hebrew printing — the *Haggadah* was included as a matter of course. It was not long, however, before it began to be printed separately. The first dated text extant is that of Fano, 1505; but it is by no means certain that it is actually the earliest. In any case it was the forerunner of a mighty tribe. By the beginning of the present century a painstaking bibliographer was able to list no less than 895 separate editions, and there can be little doubt that the total has by now exceeded a thousand.

Illustrated Editions

The very earliest published editions of the *Haggadah* made no attempt to compete with the illuminated manuscript. It was not long, however, before the tradition of the latter began to penetrate the printing-press. The earliest of all illustrated editions, of which only a fragment survives, dates from the first years of the sixteenth century, if not earlier. The most ancient complete text surviving is that produced by Gershom Cohen at Prague in 1527, which is generally known as the first illustrated *Haggadah*. This is a stately quarto

xvi

of eighty-five pages, three with exquisite borders, and profusely illustrated throughout with woodcuts. It is a magnificent example of German workmanship of the period at its finest, and perhaps remains to-day the most splendid production of the Hebrew press.

The example thus set was naturally followed in Italy — the greatest centre of Hebrew book-production and the home of Jewish art. In 1560 there was published at Mantua an illuminated *Haggadah* in close imitation of its Bohemian precursor. The work is, truth to tell, a trifle disappointing. The prototype is somewhat slavishly followed, though there are a few differences of detail to meet local conditions. Thus the boat in which the Patriarch is represented as crossing the river (in illustration of the passage 'And I took your father Abraham from beyond the River') is here converted into something suspiciously resembling a gondola! Later, this publication was in turn adapted in an edition which appeared at Venice, at that time the main centre of Hebrew printing. This was produced in different issues for the benefit of the Jews following the Spanish, the German, and the Italian rites respectively, and was republished time after time during the following centuries. Each illustration was accompanied by a descriptive rhymed couplet in Italian doggerel, printed in Hebrew characters, behind which there is similarly a long history. This edition served as the prototype for the *Haggadoth* according to the usage of the Spanish Jews which have continued to be printed down to the present day — notably at Leghorn — with the same series of illustrations, deteriorating more and more with every issue.

In 1711 an edition appeared at Amsterdam, under the auspices of the famous publishing house of Proops, which maintained an almost unceasing activity from the middle of the seventeenth to the middle of the nineteenth century. This was the first edition to make use of improved methods, being illustrated by copperplates. These were similarly based closely, though not slavishly, upon those of the Venice editions of the previous century, which had become almost classical, and are a very creditable specimen of contemporary crafts-manship. But, unfortunately, the Amsterdam edition was made to serve as the prototype of the *Haggadoth* of the German Jews and their neighbours, produced in countries where technical ability and artistic taste were at a low ebb. Its illustrations have continued to be reproduced down to our own days with increasing degree of crudity and indistinctness in every cheap Hebrew press in Europe and America, with deplorable results. One or the other of these editions served as the prototype of almost every illustrated edition of the *Haggadah* until recent years, when Joseph Budko and others led a revolt from tradition — not always with satisfactory results.

Thus, in the overwhelming majority of these *Haggadoth*, there may be discerned a regular cycle of illustrations, which may be traced back through the classical editions of Venice and Amsterdam to their Mantua and Prague prototypes, and so ultimately to the older tradition of the MSS. This same influence is to be perceived to a certain extent even in the ultra-modern editions recently produced in France, in Germany, and in England. The work is frequently prefaced by two full-page illustrations which depict, in a dozen or more panels, the preparations for the Passover and the various stages of the *Seder*. In the body of the work the illustrations may be divided into two sections. In the first part there are representations of the events spoken of in the *Haggadah* — the Rabbis discoursing at Bene Berak, the Four Sons, etc. — together with the events of the Exodus and of the lives of the Patriarchs, as mentioned in the text. A full page, sometimes a trifle realistic, would usually be devoted to the Ten Plagues. In the second half of the service the treatment changes. The atmosphere of the illustrations, like that of the text, tends to become more

Messianic. We are regaled with representations of King David at Prayer, of Jerusalem, and of the Temple. A regular tradition may be seen running through the whole of the venerable line, down sometimes to the least detail. From the first illuminated *Haggadah* that thought fit to depict the Four Sons down to the latest product of the modernistic school, the Wicked Son has almost invariably been represented as a soldier — a striking commentary upon the Jew's attitude towards war! Legend and folk-lore find their expression in the illustrations no less than history and actuality (for, it may be remarked incidentally, some of the representations form a valuable commentary upon the social life of past ages). In older editions a common subject for illustration was the bath taken by Pharaoh in the blood of Hebrew children — an ancient Rabbinic elaboration of the Biblical story, which has interesting parallels in secular lore. Generally, the Egyptian soothsayers are represented with black faces — an obvious reflection of the folk-etymology which derived the word 'negromancer' from the Latin *niger* (black), instead of the Greek νεκρός (corpse). All this goes to emphasize one fact. In the course of centuries, the illustration of the *Haggadah* — alone in the whole range of Jewish literature — became an accepted tradition. By 1900, close upon two hundred illustrated editions had appeared; and in the years that have since elapsed the total has greatly increased.

COMMENTARIES

The Jew invariably gave tangible manifestation to his affection for any particular work by loading it with commentary. By this criterion it may be said that the *Haggadah* is, perhaps, the most popular of all Jewish works after the Bible. All of the four methods of interpretation of the Talmudic and Dantesque 'Paradise' — literal, allegorical, anagogical, and moral — were lavished upon it in unparalleled profusion. Dozens of Rabbinic expositors took it in their stride while interpreting the prayer-book. Many others devoted special treatises to it. The great Rashi himself, in the eleventh century, devoted special attention to it in his (perhaps apocryphal) *Sepher haOrah*. Even Don Isaac Abrabanel, financier and diplomat, whose services were eagerly sought by the governments of Spain, Portugal, Naples, and Venice, did not disdain to turn his attention to the interpretation of this seemingly simple work — a task which he performed at unconscionable length. His commentary was deemed of such importance that it was republished time after time, was discussed by weighty authorities, and was abbreviated for more general and convenient consultation by more than one eminent writer, including Leone da Modena of Venice, the friend of Wotton and correspondent of Selden. The commentaries soon demanded super-commentaries, and *variorum* editions weighed down under their burden began to appear in the middle of the sixteenth century. Many issues present a tiny island of text in the midst of a vast surrounding sea of exposition, which in certain pages has submerged it altogether. The Vilna edition of 1892 contains no less than 115 commentaries. A recent New York compilation has rivalled that record.

TRANSLATIONS

Translations, of course, exist in all languages. Early authorities lauded the practice of interpreting the ritual into the vernacular as the service proceeded; and the case is adduced of a certain London Rabbi of the Middle Ages who used to translate the whole service (no doubt, into Norman-French) on behalf of the children and women-folk of his household. As early as 1512 a version was printed in Latin for the benefit of non-Jews — a

xviii

striking illustration of the general interest taken in this ritual. Published translations exist in Judæo-German, in Judæo-Spanish, and in Judæo-Italian (all printed in Hebrew characters), as well as in all the languages of modern Europe. The German Jews were accustomed to chant the hymn *Addir Hu* in their own tongue; while *Had Gadya* is to be found in a French version in use amongst the Jews of Bayonne, and in an old Provençal rendering which was sung by the Jews of Avignon and the Comtat Venaissin. Complete editions, without any Hebrew text, have been printed in English for the benefit of the British troops in India, and in Portuguese for the use of the Marranos in the Peninsula. Revised versions intended to appeal to the modern spirit have been published recently in England, Germany, and America.

History in the Haggadah

What a history some of the ancient copies of the work must have! In an ordinary volume, immaculateness may be a source of pride: in a *Haggadah* it is a proof of neglect. It is impossible for the time-honoured ceremonial, with its eating and its drinking, to be performed over the open volume without leaving some trace. Accordingly, any copy which can lay claim to a certain degree of antiquity almost invariably shows tangible signs of use, which speak eloquently across the intervening gulf of years. The passages at which the goblet is lifted are frequently wine-stained; at the point where the meal begins, crumbs of *Mazzah*, baked long centuries since, lie thick; and, at the end, one may find a fragment of the *Aphikoman*, put away here for luck by aged fingers which had no opportunity to take it out in the succeeding year. What scenes these marks of age recall! One may imagine some distant Ghetto, with the whole of a numerous family gathered round the *Seder* board, free men on this evening at least. The celebrant — some great scholar, perhaps, of the olden time — is conducting the service, surrounded by more than one generation of his descendants, his trembling fingers incapable of holding the glass steady, as manifested by the wine-stains which corrode the pages. And that biggest stain of all — may it not, perhaps, indicate the terror spread within the house by the shouting of a riotous mob in the street, or perhaps even by a fatal incursion? No dead volume can be more eloquent than the *Haggadah* which bears the signs of use.

V

The Present Text

The text which is here printed is that of the Jews following the German and Polish, or Ashkenazic usage: the vast majority, that is, of the Jewish population of the English-speaking countries to-day. The differences displayed by other rites are, however, inconsiderable, being centred mainly in the Grace after meals (which may be found in the ordinary prayer-books) and in the omission of certain of the final hymns. The basis of the present text, as of all modern editions, is that of Rabbi Sabbetai the Scribe, of Przemyśl, a noted seventeenth-century scholar. A very large number of versions, both printed and manuscript, have been consulted: some very rare, one or two probably unique. The rituals of the communities of Germany, Spain, Italy, Avignon, Carpentras, Byzantium, and the Yemen; the ancient formularies of the Gaons Amram and Saadiah, of Simha of Vitry and of Moses Maimonides; sumptuous manuscripts in public and private collections — all have been drawn upon and utilized to some extent. But, above all,

is cases of doubt, the promptings of common sense and of linguistic probability have been followed. In the few passages where the present wording varies from that usually printed, it will be found that it is favoured by ancient authority as well as by inherent likelihood.

THE TRANSLATION

The translation which accompanies the text has been made afresh from the original. Naturally, as many previous versions as possible have been consulted, and ample use has been made of them. The guiding principle, however, has been a reversion to an older tradition. The endeavour has been to preserve as far as possible the music and rhythm of the Hebrew, thus making the translation easier to follow as well as to appreciate. Inevitably, therefore, a certain idiomatic quality has been sacrificed, no attempt being made to compete with the free travesty which nowadays generally masquerades as a translation. Perhaps, however, this is the method which best conveys the spirit of the original; for, in a liturgical version, inspiration should be sought rather in the majestic periods of the Anglican prayer-book than in the latest fashions of modernistic prose. Quotations from the Bible of course follow the incomparable Authorized Version of 1611, excepting in cases of manifest error or sheer necessity, when the Revised Version, the American Jewish Version, and personal predilections have been followed impartially.

No pains have been spared to perfect this edition as in the more luxurious one which preceded it, by drawing upon the best contained in previous issues. May it not be deemed unworthy of its great tradition!

CECIL ROTH

הגדה של פסח

THE PASSOVER HAGGADAH

THE
HAGGADAH

A NEW EDITION
WITH ENGLISH TRANSLATION,
INTRODUCTION, AND NOTES
BY
CECIL ROTH
WITH DRAWINGS
BY
DONIA NACHSHEN

LONDON
THE SONCINO PRESS

1934–5694

ORDER OF THE SEDER SERVICE　　סימן לסדר של פסח

On Passover eve, after the Evening Service, the Seder ceremony is observed in the home.
The table is spread with a white cover, upon which are placed the festival candles or lamp.
Before the celebrant is a platter or basket, containing three specially-baked Mazzoth, or
cakes of unleavened bread, which should be adequately covered. Upon the table are placed
the necessary condiments: a baked shank-bone, parsley or some similar greenstuff, Haroseth,
an egg, and borseradish. A bowl of salt water or vinegar is also placed on the table. (For
the significance of all these symbols, reference should be made to the Introduction.) Each person
is provided with a cup of wine. The service proceeds in the ensuing manner:

Sanctification	קַדֵּשׁ.
Lave the hands	וּרְחַץ.
'Karpas'	כַּרְפַּס.
Division of the middle *mazzah*	יַחַץ.
Recital of the *Haggadah*	מַגִּיד.
Laving of the hands	רָחְצָה.
Blessing over bread	מוֹצִיא.
Blessing over the *mazzah*	מַצָּה.
Bitter Herb	מָרוֹר.
Combining *mazzah* with Bitter Herb	כּוֹרֵךְ.
THE MEAL	שֻׁלְחָן עוֹרֵךְ.
Eating of the *Aphikoman*	צָפוּן.
Grace	בָּרֵךְ.
Hallel	הַלֵּל.
All accepted	נִרְצָה:

5

SANCTIFICATION

קדש

Taking the goblet in his hand, the Celebrant recites the following. The introductory paragraph, and the passages in italic, are added if it should be Friday evening:

GENESIS I. 31—II. 3. *And it was evening, and it was morning*
the sixth day. And the heavens and the earth were finished, and all the host of them. And on the seventh day God ended His work which He had made; and He rested on the seventh day from all His work which He had made. And God blessed the seventh day, and sanctified it: because that in it He had rested from all His work which God created and made.

וַיְהִי־עֶרֶב וַיְהִי־בֹקֶר

יוֹם הַשִּׁשִּׁי ׃ וַיְכֻלּוּ הַשָּׁמַיִם וְהָאָרֶץ וְכָל־
צְבָאָם ׃ וַיְכַל אֱלֹהִים בַּיּוֹם הַשְּׁבִיעִי מְלַאכְתּוֹ
אֲשֶׁר עָשָׂה ׃ וַיִּשְׁבֹּת בַּיּוֹם הַשְּׁבִיעִי מִכָּל־
מְלַאכְתּוֹ אֲשֶׁר עָשָׂה ׃ וַיְבָרֶךְ אֱלֹהִים אֶת־
יוֹם הַשְּׁבִיעִי וַיְקַדֵּשׁ אֹתוֹ כִּי בוֹ שָׁבַת מִכָּל־
מְלַאכְתּוֹ אֲשֶׁר בָּרָא אֱלֹהִים לַעֲשׂוֹת ׃

Blessed art Thou, O Lord, our God, King of the Universe, Creator of the Produce of the Vine.
Blessed art Thou, O Lord, our God, King of the Universe: who hast chosen us from all peoples, and hast

בָּרוּךְ אַתָּה יְיָ אֱלֹהֵינוּ מֶלֶךְ
הָעוֹלָם ׃ בּוֹרֵא פְּרִי הַגָּפֶן ׃
בָּרוּךְ אַתָּה יְיָ אֱלֹהֵינוּ מֶלֶךְ
הָעוֹלָם ׃ אֲשֶׁר בָּחַר בָּנוּ מִכָּל־
עָם ׃ וְרוֹמְמָנוּ מִכָּל־לָשׁוֹן ׃

6

exalted us above all tongues, and hast sanctified us by Thy commandments. And Thou hast given us, O Lord, our God, in love, *Sabbaths for rest and* anniversaries for rejoicing, festivals and seasons for gladness: *this Sabbath day and* this feast-day of Passover, the season of our freedom, *in love*, a holy convocation in memorial of our departure from Egypt. For in us hast Thou chosen, and us hast Thou sanctified above all peoples: and Thou hast given us as heritage Thy holy *Sabbath and* seasons *in love and in favour*, in joy and in gladness. Blessed art Thou, O Lord, who sanctifiest *the Sabbath and* Israel and the festive seasons.

וְקִדַּשְׁתָּנוּ בְּמִצְוֹתָיו ∙ וַתִּתֶּן־לָנוּ
יְיָ אֱלֹהֵינוּ בְּאַהֲבָה שַׁבָּתוֹת
לִמְנוּחָה וּמוֹעֲדִים לְשִׂמְחָה
חַגִּים וּזְמַנִּים לְשָׂשׂוֹן ∙ אֶת־יוֹם
הַשַּׁבָּת הַזֶּה וְאֶת־יוֹם חַג
הַמַּצּוֹת הַזֶּה זְמַן חֵרוּתֵנוּ
בְּאַהֲבָה מִקְרָא־קֹדֶשׁ זֵכֶר
לִיצִיאַת מִצְרָיִם ∙ כִּי בָנוּ בָחַרְתָּ
וְאוֹתָנוּ קִדַּשְׁתָּ מִכָּל־הָעַמִּים
וְשַׁבָּת וּמוֹעֲדֵי קָדְשֶׁךָ בְּאַהֲבָה
וּבְרָצוֹן בְּשִׂמְחָה וּבְשָׂשׂוֹן
הִנְחַלְתָּנוּ ∙ בָּרוּךְ אַתָּה יְיָ
מְקַדֵּשׁ הַשַּׁבָּת וְיִשְׂרָאֵל
וְהַזְּמַנִּים:

The following is added if it should be Saturday night:

Blessed art thou, O Lord, our God, King of the Universe, Creator of the light of fire.
Blessed art Thou, O Lord, our God, King of the Universe, who makest distinction between holy and profane, between light and darkness, between Israel and the nations, between the seventh day and the six days of toil. Thou hast made distinction between the sanctity of the Sabbath and the sanctity of the Festival, and hast sanctified the seventh day above the six days of toil: Thou hast

בָּרוּךְ אַתָּה יְיָ אֱלֹהֵינוּ מֶלֶךְ הָעוֹלָם ∙
בּוֹרֵא מְאוֹרֵי הָאֵשׁ:
בָּרוּךְ אַתָּה יְיָ אֱלֹהֵינוּ מֶלֶךְ הָעוֹלָם ∙
הַמַּבְדִּיל בֵּין קֹדֶשׁ לְחוֹל ∙ בֵּין אוֹר לְחֹשֶׁךְ ∙
בֵּין יִשְׂרָאֵל לָעַמִּים ∙ בֵּין יוֹם הַשְּׁבִיעִי
לְשֵׁשֶׁת יְמֵי הַמַּעֲשֶׂה: בֵּין קְדֻשַּׁת שַׁבָּת
לִקְדֻשַּׁת יוֹם טוֹב הִבְדַּלְתָּ וְאֶת־יוֹם

7

distinguished and sanctified Thy people Israel with Thine own sanctity. Blessed art Thou, O Lord, who makest distinction between holy and holy.

הַשְּׁבִיעִי מִשֵּׁשֶׁת יְמֵי־הַמַּעֲשֶׂה קִדָּשְׁתָּ. הִבְדַּלְתָּ וְקִדַּשְׁתָּ אֶת־עַמְּךָ יִשְׂרָאֵל בִּקְדֻשָּׁתֶךָ. בָּרוּךְ אַתָּה יְיָ הַמַּבְדִּיל בֵּין קֹדֶשׁ לְקֹדֶשׁ:

Blessed art Thou, O Lord, our God, King of the Universe, who hast preserved us and sustained us and enabled us to reach this season.

בָּרוּךְ אַתָּה יְיָ אֱלֹהֵינוּ מֶלֶךְ הָעוֹלָם. שֶׁהֶחֱיָנוּ וְקִיְּמָנוּ וְהִגִּיעָנוּ לַזְּמַן הַזֶּה:

The first cup of wine is here drunk.

LAVE THE HANDS ורחץ

The Celebrant (but not the rest of the company) here rinses his hands: an obvious piece of hygiene before the next stage in the proceedings, and an excellent illustration of the fact, of which we are reminded more than once in the course of the Seder, that, in Judaism, cleanliness is an integral part of godliness.

'KARPAS' כרפס

The Celebrant distributes a fragment of the 'Karpas', dipped in salt water or in vinegar. The following benediction is recited before eating it:

Blessed art Thou, O Lord, our God, King of the Universe, Creator of the Produce of the Earth.

בָּרוּךְ אַתָּה יְיָ אֱלֹהֵינוּ מֶלֶךְ הָעוֹלָם. בּוֹרֵא פְּרִי הָאֲדָמָה:

KARPAS: Before the meal is begun, hors-d'œuvre is distributed, of the species general for the purpose a couple of thousand years ago, when the *Seder* was fixed: naturally, something of a slightly pungent flavour, steeped in some liquid of a similar nature. This ultimately became symbolically identified with the bunch of hyssop which was dipped in the blood of the first Paschal sacrifice at the time of the Exodus and used for marking the doorways of the houses of the children of Israel, as a sign to the Angel of Death. *Karpas* is defined as 'an umbelliferous plant', an umbelliferous plant being 'a flower-cluster in which stalks nearly equal in length spring from a common centre and form a flat or convex or concave surface. The herb usually employed is parsley: though lettuce, carrot-tops, etc. will serve equally well.

8

DIVISION

יחץ

The Celebrant breaks into two the middle Mazzah of the three on the tray before him. One portion he leaves where it is, for later consumption. The larger section, which is known as the 'Aphikoman', is put away somewhere about the room — generally either under the table-cloth or else between the cushions upon which he is supported.

RECITAL OF THE HAGGADAH

מגיד

At this stage, it is customary to remove the egg and the bone and to uncover the Mazzoth upon which attention is thereby concentrated. The tray is then lifted up and displayed to the company, of whom those who are nearest put out their hands to assist in supporting it, while the Celebrant recites the following formula:

This is the bread of affliction that our fathers ate in the land of Egypt. All who are hungered—let them come and eat: all who are needy—let them come and celebrate the Passover. Now we are here, but next year may we be in the land of Israel! Now we are slaves, but next year may we be free men!

הָא לַחְמָא עַנְיָא דִי־אֲכָלוּ
אַבְהָתָנָא בְּאַרְעָא דְמִצְרָיִם.
כָּל־דִכְפִין יֵיתֵי וְיֵכוֹל. כָּל־
דִצְרִיךְ יֵיתֵי וְיִפְסַח. הָשַׁתָּא
הָכָא. לְשָׁנָה הַבָּאָה בְּאַרְעָא
דְיִשְׂרָאֵל. הָשַׁתָּא עַבְדֵי.
לְשָׁנָה הַבָּאָה בְּנֵי חוֹרִין:

RECITAL OF THE HAGGADAH: The passage above is amongst the very oldest in the *Haggadah*. It is written, not in Hebrew, but in Aramaic — the language actually spoken amongst the Jewish people in Palestine in the centuries immediately before and after the beginning of the Christian era. The reference to the celebration of the Passover (i.e. partaking of the Paschal sacrifice) indicates clearly that it antedates the destruction of the Temple: and it has indeed been conjectured that the recital was composed in Mesopotamia during the Captivity, in the sixth century before the current era. The invitation to all who are hungry to come and eat is not a barren formula. The Jew who refuses hospitality to a needy coreligionist on this night is false to the whole spirit of the observance.

Wherein is this night different from all other nights? For, on all other nights, we may eat either leavened bread or unleavened, but on this night only unleavened: on all other nights we may eat other kinds of herb, but on this night only bitter herbs: on all other nights we need not dip our herbs even once, but on this night we do so twice: on all other nights we eat either sitting upright or reclining, but on this night we all recline.

מַה־נִּשְׁתַּנָּה הַלַּיְלָה הַזֶּה
מִכָּל־הַלֵּילוֹת. שֶׁבְּכָל־הַלֵּילוֹת
אָנוּ אוֹכְלִין חָמֵץ וּמַצָּה,
הַלַּיְלָה הַזֶּה כֻּלּוֹ מַצָּה: שֶׁבְּכָל־
הַלֵּילוֹת אָנוּ אוֹכְלִין שְׁאָר
יְרָקוֹת. הַלַּיְלָה הַזֶּה מָרוֹר:
שֶׁבְּכָל־הַלֵּילוֹת אֵין אָנוּ
מַטְבִּילִין אֲפִילוּ פַּעַם אֶחָת.
הַלַּיְלָה הַזֶּה שְׁתֵּי פְעָמִים:
שֶׁבְּכָל־הַלֵּילוֹת אָנוּ אוֹכְלִין
בֵּין יוֹשְׁבִין וּבֵין מְסֻבִּין. הַלַּיְלָה
הַזֶּה כֻּלָּנוּ מְסֻבִּין:

THE FOUR QUESTIONS: The division of the middle *Mazzah*, the lifting of the dish, and the recital of the Aramaic formula just ended may be calculated to arouse the curiosity of any normal child. Accordingly, here are asked the questions in response to which the formal 'telling' (*Haggadah*) may take place. Not that these must necessarily follow any fixed form. It is recounted that the little daughter of one famous Rabbi, her interest attracted by the raising of the dish, inquired of her father why he had acted in this manner. The latter went straight on to the formal recital of the answer, considering this spontaneous question sufficient. The *Mishnah*, however, compiled in the second century, suggests four questions which the child might be expected to ask. This formula, slightly adapted for modern conditions, still serves us to-day. There is only one difference of any importance. While the Temple was standing, and the Paschal lamb actually offered, the question was asked why, on this night, the meat was roasted only, and not sodden or boiled. This is now replaced by the inquiry about leaning. This, and the eating of the *Mazzah*, have previously been made evident: while the child knows that only bitter herbs are used, and that they are 'dipped' twice (once, already, in the salt water or vinegar, in the case of the *Karpas*: the second time later on, when the Bitter Herb is tempered with *Haroseth*) because of the preparations on the table, which, it may be imagined, have already attracted attention.

The questions are usually asked by the youngest child at table, boy or girl: if there are no children, by the youngest individual present. Where husband and wife are alone together, the wife asks her husband: and, in those cases when a person is compelled to perform the ceremonial all alone, he should read the questions himself.

The Mazzoth are uncovered, and the Celebrant replies:

'We were Pharaoh's bond-men in Egypt: and the Lord our God brought us out therefrom with a mighty hand' (Deut. vi. 21) and an out-stretched arm. Now, if the Holy One, blessed be He, had

עֲבָדִים הָיִינוּ לְפַרְעֹה בְּמִצְרָיִם · וַיּוֹצִיאֵנוּ יְיָ אֱלֹהֵינוּ מִשָּׁם בְּיָד חֲזָקָה וּבִזְרוֹעַ נְטוּיָה: וְאִלּוּ לֹא הוֹצִיא הַקָּדוֹשׁ

THE ANSWER: The answer of the father follows a tradition hardly less ancient than the questions themselves. The Mishnah in its instructions is content with laying down the general prescription: 'The Father instructs his son according to his capacity, beginning with shame and ending with praise: and he expounds from *A Syrian would have destroyed my Father* (Deuteronomy xxvi. 5) until he ends the whole passage.' This exposition comes a little later on in the service. For what leads up to it there were reported in the Talmud, in its commentary upon the Mishnah, two different traditions. Both of these are embodied in the ritual as we have it to-day. The formula here given follows the recommendations of Samuel, the great Mesopotamian authority of the third century, and one of the most eminent rabbinical scholars of his age. It is based upon Deuteronomy vi. 21, of which the opening passage is an almost verbal quotation. The 'shame' with which it starts is an allusion to the servitude.

11

not brought our fathers forth from Egypt, then we, and our children, and our children's children, would be servants to Pharaoh in Egypt. Therefore, even were we all wise, all men of understanding, all advanced in years, and all endowed with knowledge of the Torah, it would nevertheless be our duty to tell the story of the coming forth from Egypt: and the more a man tells of the coming forth from Egypt, the more is he to be praised.

It is told of Rabbi Eliezer, Rabbi Joshua, Rabbi Eleazar, son of Azariah, Rabbi Akiba, and Rabbi Tarphon, that

בָּרוּךְ הוּא אֶת־אֲבוֹתֵינוּ מִמִּצְרַיִם. הֲרֵי אָנוּ וּבָנֵינוּ וּבְנֵי בָנֵינוּ מְשֻׁעְבָּדִים הָיִינוּ לְפַרְעֹה בְּמִצְרָיִם. וַאֲפִילוּ כֻּלָּנוּ חֲכָמִים. כֻּלָּנוּ נְבוֹנִים. כֻּלָּנוּ זְקֵנִים. כֻּלָּנוּ יוֹדְעִים אֶת־הַתּוֹרָה. מִצְוָה עָלֵינוּ לְסַפֵּר בִּיצִיאַת מִצְרָיִם. וְכָל־הַמַּרְבֶּה לְסַפֵּר בִּיצִיאַת מִצְרַיִם הֲרֵי זֶה מְשֻׁבָּח:

מַעֲשֶׂה בְּרַבִּי אֱלִיעֶזֶר וְרַבִּי יְהוֹשֻׁעַ וְרַבִּי אֶלְעָזָר בֶּן־עֲזַרְיָה וְרַבִּי עֲקִיבָא וְרַבִּי טַרְפוֹן

THE FIVE SAGES: After an exposition in general terms of the reason for recounting the story of the Exodus, there comes an actual instance shewing that the duty is incumbent upon all, however advanced in years and learning. The five Rabbis in question were among the most eminent of the second century, in the generation following the fall of the Jewish state. Best known of them is Akiba, the paladin of the Talmud, whose school was situated at Bene Berak, south-east of Jaffa. He it was, in all probability, who was the host on this occasion. So absorbed were he and his companions in their tale, that they did not notice the passage of time, and their pupils had to come and remind them that the hour for the morning prayer had arrived (the *Shema* consists of the Biblical passages Deuteronomy vi. 4—9, xi. 13—21, Numbers xv. 37—41, which form the kernel of both morning and evening service: it is called after the initial word, *Hear!*). The conjecture has been made that these eminent Rabbis went on from recounting the story of the redemption from Egypt to a discussion of the prospects of deliverance from the Roman tyranny. This would explain their meeting together in one place and their absorption in the subject, as well as the apparent exclusion of their disciples. As a matter of fact, within a few years there broke out the Bar Kochba rebellion, which for a time threatened the Roman rule in Palestine. In its suppression, the school of Bene Berak was broken up, Jewish life in the southern part of the country was threatened with extinction, and Akiba met a martyr's death (135).

This interesting passage is in full Mishnaic style, and is to be found in no other source. It obviously dates back to a period only slightly posterior to that of which it speaks — to the close, that is, of the second century. In the Tosefta, a contemporary compilation (*Pesahim* cap. x), a similar story is told of Rabban Gamaliel the Patriarch and the elders, at Lydda.

they were once reclining together at Bene Berak, and they were recounting the story of the coming forth from Egypt all that night, until their pupils came and said to them: 'Our Masters! The time has come for reciting the morning prayer.'

שֶׁהָיוּ מְסֻבִּין בִּבְנֵי בְרַק. וְהָיוּ מְסַפְּרִים בִּיצִיאַת מִצְרַיִם כָּל־אוֹתוֹ הַלַּיְלָה. עַד־שֶׁבָּאוּ תַלְמִידֵיהֶם וְאָמְרוּ לָהֶם. רַבּוֹתֵינוּ. הִגִּיעַ זְמַן קְרִיאַת שְׁמַע שֶׁל־שַׁחֲרִית:

DONIA NACHSHEN

13

R. Eleazar, b. Azariah, said: 'Now, I am as seventy years of age, yet I did not understand why the coming forth from Egypt should be told at night until Ben Zoma explained it: It is said, "That thou mayest remember the day when thou camest forth from the land of Egypt all the days of thy life" (Deut. xvi. 3). "The days of thy life" would imply the days only: "*all* the days of thy life" includes the nights also. The sages, however, expound it thus: "The days of thy life" refers to this world: "*all* the days of thy life" is to include the days of the Messiah.'

Blessed be the All-Present, blessed be He: Blessed be He who gave the law to His people Israel, blessed be He.

With reference to four sons doth the Torah speak: one wise, one wicked, one simple, and one who does not know how to ask.

אָמַר רַבִּי אֶלְעָזָר בֶּן־עֲזַרְיָה.
הֲרֵי אֲנִי כְּבֶן־שִׁבְעִים שָׁנָה.
וְלֹא זָכִיתִי שֶׁתֵּאָמֵר יְצִיאַת
מִצְרַיִם בַּלֵּילוֹת. עַד שֶׁדְּרָשָׁהּ
בֶּן־זוֹמָא. שֶׁנֶּאֱמַר: לְמַעַן
תִּזְכֹּר אֶת־יוֹם צֵאתְךָ מֵאֶרֶץ
מִצְרַיִם כָּל יְמֵי חַיֶּיךָ: יְמֵי חַיֶּיךָ
הַיָּמִים. כָּל יְמֵי חַיֶּיךָ הַלֵּילוֹת.
וַחֲכָמִים אוֹמְרִים יְמֵי חַיֶּיךָ
הָעוֹלָם הַזֶּה. כָּל יְמֵי חַיֶּיךָ
לְהָבִיא לִימוֹת הַמָּשִׁיחַ:

בָּרוּךְ הַמָּקוֹם. בָּרוּךְ הוּא.
בָּרוּךְ שֶׁנָּתַן תּוֹרָה לְעַמּוֹ
יִשְׂרָאֵל. בָּרוּךְ הוּא:

כְּנֶגֶד אַרְבָּעָה בָנִים דִּבְּרָה
תוֹרָה. אֶחָד חָכָם. וְאֶחָד
רָשָׁע. וְאֶחָד תָּם. וְאֶחָד שֶׁאֵינוֹ
יוֹדֵעַ לִשְׁאוֹל:

'BLESSED BE THE ALL-PRESENT': The next passage is introduced by a simple benedictory formula preparatory to the exposition of a passage from the Law. The phrase *makom*, or 'Place', used as a denomination of the Deity (here rendered as 'All-Present'), is explained in the famous apophthegm: 'He is the Place of the world, yet the world is not His place'. The fourfold occurrence in it of the word 'blessed' was afterwards taken as referring to the four sons mentioned immediately afterwards: for (as some later authorities semi-jocularly put it) a man should bless God for the evil no less than for the good!

The Wise Son—what does he say? 'What mean the testimonies and the statutes and the judgements which the Lord our God hath commanded you?' (Deut. vi. 20) Thou must similarly expound to him the laws of the Passover, even that we do not dismiss the company after the Passover Meal for entertainment.

חָכָם מָה הוּא אוֹמֵר. מָה
הָעֵדוֹת וְהַחֻקִּים וְהַמִּשְׁפָּטִים
אֲשֶׁר צִוָּה יְיָ אֱלֹהֵינוּ אֶתְכֶם:
וְאַף אַתָּה אֱמֹר לוֹ כְּהִלְכוֹת
הַפֶּסַח. אֵין מַפְטִירִין אַחַר
הַפֶּסַח אֲפִיקוֹמָן:

The four sons: Four times in the Pentateuch (Ex. XII. 26; XIII. 8, 14; Deut. VI. 20) we find mentioned a man's duty to recount the story of the Exodus to his son on the occasion of the Passover. The Torah can contain, *ex hypothesi*, no useless duplication: and the Rabbis accordingly discovered in the phraseology of the various texts allusion to four different types of child — the intelligent, who desires to learn; the petulant, who asks as though everything is a burden; the immature, who can do no more than inquire the reason for any unusual procedure; and the infant who has not even got to the asking stage, and must have everything explained to him. The description of the four types, their questions, and the corresponding answers, displays a good deal of humour as well as of psychological insight: and they have formed a favourite subject for the illustrators of the *Haggadah* from earliest times. It is noteworthy, as a clue to the Jewish temperament, that the Wicked Son is always depicted as a soldier. The passage is copied from the Palestinian Talmud (*Pesahim,* f. 34, where a parallel seems to be drawn between the four sons and the four goblets). There are, however, one or two slight but significant alterations — e.g. the Foolish Son of the original has now become merely simple! The Wise Son (the simple one, according to the original text: standards of intelligence have apparently changed!) receives as his reward a detailed description of the laws concerning the Passover, down to the least detail: e.g. 'We do not break up the Passover meal by saying ἐπὶ κῶμον — *to the after-dinner entertainment!*' The interpretation of this passage has been rendered obscure by the similarity of the phrase here used with *Aphikoman*, spoken of above, which, though derived from the same Greek words, means something totally different. The law referred to is to be found in the Mishnah, *Pesahim* x. 8. The gloss of the Palestinian Talmud to the passage renders the interpretation beyond reasonable doubt: that a man should not be in one company and go to join another — the regular musical conclusion to a banquet in classical times. The difficulty has been raised that the Wise Son, no

15

The Wicked Son—what does he say? 'What mean ye by this service?' (Ex. xii. 26) 'Ye', he insinuates, not himself. Since he has excluded himself from the generality, he has denied a cardinal principle. Therefore shouldst thou also distress him, saying, 'It is because of that which the Lord did for me when I came forth from Egypt' (Ex. xiii. 8): for *me*, not for him—for if he had been there, he would not have been redeemed!

The Simple Son—what does he say? 'What is this?' (Ex. xiii. 14) And thou shalt say unto him, 'By strength of hand the Lord brought us out of the Land of Egypt, from the house of bondage.' (*Ibid.*)

רָשָׁע מָה הוּא אוֹמֵר. מָה הָעֲבוֹדָה הַזֹּאת לָכֶם: לָכֶם וְלֹא לוֹ. וּלְפִי שֶׁהוֹצִיא אֶת עַצְמוֹ מִן־הַכְּלָל כָּפַר בְּעִקָּר: וְאַף אַתָּה הַקְהֵה אֶת־שִׁנָּיו וֶאֱמֹר לוֹ. בַּעֲבוּר זֶה עָשָׂה יְיָ לִי בְּצֵאתִי מִמִּצְרָיִם: לִי וְלֹא לוֹ. אִלּוּ הָיָה שָׁם לֹא הָיָה נִגְאָל:

תָּם מָה הוּא אוֹמֵר. מַה־זֹּאת. וְאָמַרְתָּ אֵלָיו. בְּחֹזֶק יָד הוֹצִיאָנוּ יְיָ מִמִּצְרַיִם מִבֵּית עֲבָדִים:

less than his wicked brother, refers to the duties incumbent upon 'you' (in the second person). His inquiry is, however, obviously intended to elicit information. The other is purely contemptuous, using 'service' in the sense of 'servitude'.

g

As for him who does not know how to ask, thou shalt thyself begin for him, as it is said: 'And thou shalt tell thy son in that day, saying, It is because of that which the Lord did for me when I came forth out of Egypt.' (Ex. xiii. 8)

וְשֶׁאֵינוֹ יוֹדֵעַ לִשְׁאוֹל אַתְּ פְּתַח לוֹ. שֶׁנֶּאֱמַר: וְהִגַּדְתָּ לְבִנְךָ בַּיּוֹם הַהוּא לֵאמֹר. בַּעֲבוּר זֶה עָשָׂה יְיָ לִי בְּצֵאתִי מִמִּצְרָיִם:

It might be thought that this exposition should begin from the New Moon of Nisan. The text says, however, 'in that day'. If it is to be 'in that day', it might be thought that the exposition should begin in the daytime; but the text

יָכוֹל מֵרֹאשׁ חֹדֶשׁ. תַּלְמוּד לוֹמַר בַּיּוֹם הַהוּא. אִי בַּיּוֹם הַהוּא יָכוֹל מִבְּעוֹד יוֹם. תַּלְמוּד לוֹמַר בַּעֲבוּר זֶה. בַּעֲבוּר זֶה

It is on the exposition to the son who does not know how to ask that the main portion of the *Haggadah* is based. The ritual therefore goes on to shew, by a characteristic piece of Talmudic reasoning, that this formality is to take place on the Passover eve — not from the beginning of the month, when preparations commence, nor yet in the afternoon, at the time of the Paschal sacrifice. This passage, which is to be found in the *Mekhilta* to the verse, leads on to the prescribed 'telling', or *Haggadah* proper.

'IN THE BEGINNING': From this point, after it has been shewn that all persons must recount the story of the Exodus, and that the duty is incumbent precisely on the Passover eve, the heart of the 'telling' is reached: beginning (according to the ancient formula) with shame and ending with praise.

The opening passage is according to the tradition of Abba Arikha ('Rab'), a famous Babylonian scholar of the third century, being his alternative to 'We were Pharaoh's bondmen in Egypt' prescribed by his contemporary, Samuel.

17

says 'because of that'. 'Because of *that*' I would not have said, except with reference to the time when unleavened bread and bitter herb are laid before thee.

In the beginning, our Fathers were worshippers of strange gods: but now the All-Present has brought us to His service, as it is said: 'And Joshua said unto all the people, Thus saith the Lord God of Israel, Your fathers dwelt of old time beyond the River, even Terah, the father of Abraham and the father of Nahor: and they served other gods. And I took your father Abraham from beyond the River, and led him throughout all the land of Canaan, and multiplied his seed, and gave him Isaac. And I gave unto Isaac, Jacob and Esau; and I gave unto Esau, Mount Seir, to possess it; and Jacob and his children went down into Egypt.' (Jos. xxiv. 2—4)

Blessed be He who observes His promise to Israel: blessed be He! For the Holy One, blessed be He, determined the end of the bondage in

לֹא אָמַרְתִּי אֶלָּא בְּשָׁעָה שֶׁיֵּשׁ
מַצָּה וּמָרוֹר מֻנָּחִים לְפָנֶיךָ:

מִתְּחִלָּה עוֹבְדֵי עֲבוֹדָה זָרָה
הָיוּ אֲבוֹתֵינוּ. וְעַכְשָׁו קֵרְבָנוּ
הַמָּקוֹם לַעֲבוֹדָתוֹ. שֶׁנֶּאֱמַר:
וַיֹּאמֶר יְהוֹשֻׁעַ אֶל־כָּל־הָעָם.
כֹּה אָמַר יְיָ אֱלֹהֵי יִשְׂרָאֵל
בְּעֵבֶר הַנָּהָר יָשְׁבוּ אֲבוֹתֵיכֶם
מֵעוֹלָם תֶּרַח אֲבִי אַבְרָהָם
וַאֲבִי נָחוֹר וַיַּעַבְדוּ אֱלֹהִים
אֲחֵרִים: וָאֶקַּח אֶת־אֲבִיכֶם
אֶת־אַבְרָהָם מֵעֵבֶר הַנָּהָר.
וָאוֹלֵךְ אוֹתוֹ בְּכָל־אֶרֶץ כְּנָעַן
וָאַרְבֶּה אֶת־זַרְעוֹ וָאֶתֶּן־לוֹ
אֶת־יִצְחָק: וָאֶתֵּן לְיִצְחָק אֶת־
יַעֲקֹב וְאֶת־עֵשָׂו. וָאֶתֵּן לְעֵשָׂו
אֶת־הַר שֵׂעִיר לָרֶשֶׁת אוֹתוֹ
וְיַעֲקֹב וּבָנָיו יָרְדוּ מִצְרָיִם:

בָּרוּךְ שׁוֹמֵר הַבְטָחָתוֹ
לְיִשְׂרָאֵל. בָּרוּךְ הוּא שֶׁהַקָּדוֹשׁ
בָּרוּךְ הוּא חִשַּׁב אֶת־הַקֵּץ

18

order to fulfil that which He had said to Abraham our father in the Pact between the Portions, as it is said: 'And He said unto Abram, Know thou of a surety that thy seed shall be a stranger in a land that is not theirs, and shall serve them, and they shall afflict them, four hundred years; and also that nation, whom they shall serve, will I judge: and afterward shall they come out with great substance.' (Gen. xv. 13, 14)

לַעֲשׂוֹת כְּמָה שֶׁאָמַר לְאַבְרָהָם
אָבִינוּ בִּבְרִית בֵּין הַבְּתָרִים.
שֶׁנֶּאֱמַר: וַיֹּאמֶר לְאַבְרָם יָדֹעַ
תֵּדַע כִּי־גֵר יִהְיֶה זַרְעֲךָ בְּאֶרֶץ
לֹא לָהֶם וַעֲבָדוּם וְעִנּוּ אוֹתָם.
אַרְבַּע מֵאוֹת שָׁנָה: וְגַם אֶת־
הַגּוֹי אֲשֶׁר יַעֲבֹדוּ דָּן אָנֹכִי.
וְאַחֲרֵי־כֵן יֵצְאוּ בִּרְכֻשׁ גָּדוֹל:

Here the Goblet is raised in thanksgiving, and the Mazzoth are covered:

This faithfulness it is that has stood by our fathers and us. For not one man only has risen up against us to destroy us, but in every generation do men rise up against us to destroy us: but the Holy One, blessed be He, delivers us from their hands.

וְהִיא שֶׁעָמְדָה לַאֲבוֹתֵינוּ
וְלָנוּ. שֶׁלֹּא אֶחָד בִּלְבַד עָמַד
עָלֵינוּ לְכַלּוֹתֵנוּ. אֶלָּא שֶׁבְּכָל־
דּוֹר וָדוֹר עוֹמְדִים עָלֵינוּ
לְכַלּוֹתֵנוּ. וְהַקָּדוֹשׁ בָּרוּךְ הוּא
מַצִּילֵנוּ מִיָּדָם:

'THE PACT BETWEEN THE PORTIONS': This is the name given in Hebrew literature to the Covenant of Abraham reported in the fifteenth chapter of the book of Exodus. This plays an extremely important part in Rabbinic theology, in which reference is constantly made to it. The prominent position which it occupied in Jewish imagination in the first centuries of the Christian era may be gauged from the fact that the pseudepigraphical Apocalypse of Abraham centres upon this same mystical scene. The Four Hundred Years here mentioned do not necessarily refer exclusively to the period of the servitude of the Hebrews in Egypt, but to their residence as strangers 'in a land which was not theirs'. According to the old Jewish commentators, the beginning of this is to be reckoned from the birth of Isaac.

'THIS FAITHFULNESS IT IS': A noble passage, familiar already in the ritual of the Gaon Natronai, who flourished in the ninth century.

Come and learn what Laban the Syrian sought to do to Jacob our Father. For Pharaoh issued his edict only against the males, but Laban sought to uproot all, as it is said: '*A Syrian would have destroyed my Father, and he went down to Egypt and sojourned there, few in number; and he became there a nation, great, mighty, and populous.*' (Deut. xxvi. 5, alternative rendering.)

צֵא וּלְמַד מַה־בִּקֵּשׁ לָבָן הָאֲרַמִּי לַעֲשׂוֹת לְיַעֲקֹב אָבִינוּ. שֶׁפַּרְעֹה לֹא גָזַר אֶלָּא עַל־הַזְּכָרִים. וְלָבָן בִּקֵּשׁ לַעֲקוֹר אֶת־הַכֹּל. שֶׁנֶּאֱמַר: אֲרַמִּי אֹבֵד אָבִי וַיֵּרֶד מִצְרַיְמָה וַיָּגָר שָׁם בִּמְתֵי מְעָט. וַיְהִי־שָׁם לְגוֹי גָּדוֹל עָצוּם וָרָב:

And he went down into Egypt—compelled by the Divine decree. *And sojourned there*—teaching that he did not go to settle, but to sojourn for a space, as it is said: '*They said moreover unto Pharaoh, For to sojourn in the land are we come, for thy servants have no pasture for their flocks, for the famine is sore in the land of Canaan: now therefore, we pray thee, let thy servants dwell in the land of Goshen.*' (Gen. xlvii. 4)

וַיֵּרֶד מִצְרַיְמָה. אָנוּס עַל־פִּי הַדִּבּוּר: וַיָּגָר שָׁם. מְלַמֵּד שֶׁלֹּא יָרַד לְהִשְׁתַּקֵּעַ בְּמִצְרַיִם אֶלָּא לָגוּר שָׁם. שֶׁנֶּאֱמַר: וַיֹּאמְרוּ אֶל־פַּרְעֹה לָגוּר בָּאָרֶץ בָּאנוּ כִּי־אֵין מִרְעֶה לַצֹּאן אֲשֶׁר לַעֲבָדֶיךָ כִּי־כָבֵד הָרָעָב בְּאֶרֶץ כְּנָעַן. וְעַתָּה יֵשְׁבוּ־נָא עֲבָדֶיךָ בְּאֶרֶץ גֹּשֶׁן:

'COME AND LEARN': We now come to an exposition, or *Midrash*, of Deuteronomy, xxvi. 5—7, as recommended in the Mishnah. This is a typical piece of Rabbinical interpretation of this sort in its simplest form. The words of Scripture are minutely analysed: their full implications are brought out: and it is shown how they are supported by other Biblical passages. It is a fine example of this species of literature, of an early date, and is found in no other source.

Few in number, as it is said:
'Thy fathers went down into
Egypt with three-score and
ten persons; and now the
Lord thy God hath made
thee as the stars of heaven
for multitude.' (Deut. x. 22) *And
he became there a nation*: teaching that Israel was distinguished there. *Great, mighty*:
as it is said: 'And the children of Israel were fruitful,
and increased abundantly,
and multiplied, and waxed
exceeding mighty; and the
land was filled with them'.
(Ex. 1. 7)

בִּמְתֵי מְעָט · כְּמָה שֶׁנֶּאֱמַר:
בְּשִׁבְעִים נֶפֶשׁ יָרְדוּ אֲבֹתֶיךָ
מִצְרָיְמָה · וְעַתָּה שָׂמְךָ יְיָ
אֱלֹהֶיךָ כְּכוֹכְבֵי הַשָּׁמַיִם לָרֹב:
וַיְהִי־שָׁם לְגוֹי · מְלַמֵּד שֶׁהָיוּ
יִשְׂרָאֵל מְצֻיָּנִין שָׁם: גָּדוֹל
עָצוּם · כְּמָה שֶׁנֶּאֱמַר · וּבְנֵי
יִשְׂרָאֵל פָּרוּ וַיִּשְׁרְצוּ וַיִּרְבּוּ
וַיַּעַצְמוּ בִּמְאֹד מְאֹד · וַתִּמָּלֵא
הָאָרֶץ אֹתָם:

And populous, as it is said: 'I
caused thee to multiply as
the bud of the field, and thou
didst increase and wax great,
and thou attainedst to excellent ornaments; thy breasts
were fashioned, and thine
hair was grown: yet thou wast
naked and bare.' (Ezek. xvi. 7)

וָרָב · כְּמָה שֶׁנֶּאֱמַר: רְבָבָה
כְּצֶמַח הַשָּׂדֶה נְתַתִּיךְ וַתִּרְבִּי
וַתִּגְדְּלִי וַתָּבֹאִי בַּעֲדִי עֲדָיִים ·
שָׁדַיִם נָכֹנוּ וּשְׂעָרֵךְ צִמֵּחַ וְאַתְּ
עֵרֹם וְעֶרְיָה:

*And the Egyptians evil en-
treated us, and afflicted us, and
laid upon us hard bondage.* (Deut.
xxvi. 6)

וַיָּרֵעוּ אֹתָנוּ הַמִּצְרִים וַיְעַנּוּנוּ ·
וַיִּתְּנוּ עָלֵינוּ עֲבֹדָה קָשָׁה:

*And the Egyptians evil en-
treated us*, as it is said, 'Come
on, let us deal wisely with
them; lest they multiply, and
it come to pass, that, when

וַיָּרֵעוּ אֹתָנוּ הַמִּצְרִים · כְּמָה
שֶׁנֶּאֱמַר: הָבָה נִתְחַכְּמָה לוֹ ·
פֶּן־יִרְבֶּה וְהָיָה כִּי־תִקְרֶאנָה

there falleth out any war, they also join themselves unto our enemies, and fight against us, and get them up out of the land.' (Ex. i. 10)

And afflicted us, as it is said, 'Therefore they did set over them taskmasters to afflict them with their burdens. And they built for Pharaoh treasure cities, Pithom and Rameses.' (Ex. i. 11)

מִלְחָמָה וְנוֹסַף גַּם־הוּא עַל־שֹׂנְאֵינוּ וְנִלְחַם־בָּנוּ וְעָלָה מִן הָאָרֶץ:

וַיְעַנּוּנוּ ‧ כְּמָה שֶׁנֶּאֱמַר: וַיָּשִׂימוּ עָלָיו שָׂרֵי מִסִּים לְמַעַן עַנֹּתוֹ בְּסִבְלֹתָם ‧ וַיִּבֶן עָרֵי מִסְכְּנוֹת לְפַרְעֹה אֶת־פִּתֹם וְאֶת־רַעַמְסֵס:

And laid upon us hard bondage, as it is said: 'And the Egyptians made the children of Israel to serve with rigour.' (Ex. i. 13)

וַיִּתְּנוּ עָלֵינוּ עֲבֹדָה קָשָׁה. כְּמָה שֶׁנֶּאֱמַר: וַיַּעֲבִדוּ מִצְרַיִם אֶת־בְּנֵי יִשְׂרָאֵל בְּפָרֶךְ:

22

And we cried unto the Lord the God of our fathers and the Lord heard our voice and saw our affliction and our toil and our oppression. (Deut. xxvi. 7)

וַנִּצְעַק אֶל־יְיָ אֱלֹהֵי אֲבֹתֵינוּ. וַיִּשְׁמַע יְיָ אֶת־קֹלֵנוּ וַיַּרְא אֶת־עָנְיֵנוּ וְאֶת־עֲמָלֵנוּ וְאֶת־לַחֲצֵנוּ׃

And we cried unto the Lord the God of our fathers, as it is said: 'And it came to pass in the course of those many days, that the king of Egypt died: and the children of Israel sighed by reason of their bondage, and they cried, and their cry came up unto God by reason of their bondage.' (Ex. ii. 23)

וַנִּצְעַק אֶל־יְיָ אֱלֹהֵי אֲבֹתֵינוּ. כְּמָה שֶׁנֶּאֱמַר: וַיְהִי בַיָּמִים הָרַבִּים הָהֵם וַיָּמָת מֶלֶךְ מִצְרַיִם וַיֵּאָנְחוּ בְנֵי־יִשְׂרָאֵל מִן־הָעֲבֹדָה וַיִּזְעָקוּ. וַתַּעַל שַׁוְעָתָם אֶל־הָאֱלֹהִים מִן־הָעֲבֹדָה׃

And the Lord heard our voice, as it is said: 'And God heard their groaning, and God remembered His covenant with Abraham, with Isaac, and with Jacob.' (Ex. ii. 24)

וַיִּשְׁמַע יְיָ אֶת־קֹלֵנוּ. כְּמָה שֶׁנֶּאֱמַר: וַיִּשְׁמַע אֱלֹהִים אֶת־נַאֲקָתָם. וַיִּזְכֹּר אֱלֹהִים אֶת־בְּרִיתוֹ אֶת־אַבְרָהָם אֶת־יִצְחָק וְאֶת־יַעֲקֹב׃

And saw our affliction: this refers to the separation of man from wife, as it is said: 'And God saw the children of Israel, and God knew.' (Ex. ii. 25)

וַיַּרְא אֶת־עָנְיֵנוּ. זוֹ פְּרִישׁוּת דֶּרֶךְ אֶרֶץ. כְּמָה שֶׁנֶּאֱמַר: וַיַּרְא אֱלֹהִים אֶת־בְּנֵי יִשְׂרָאֵל. וַיֵּדַע אֱלֹהִים׃

And our toil: this refers to the sons, as it is said: 'Every son that is born ye shall cast into

וְאֶת־עֲמָלֵנוּ. אֵלוּ הַבָּנִים. כְּמָה שֶׁנֶּאֱמַר: כָּל־הַבֵּן הַיִּלּוֹד

23

the river, and every daughter ye shall save alive.' (Ex. i. 22)

הַיְאֹרָה תַּשְׁלִיכֻהוּ · וְכָל־הַבַּת תְּחַיּוּן :

And our oppression: this refers to the vexation, as it is said, 'Moreover, I have seen the oppression wherewith the Egyptians oppress them.' (Ex. iii. 9)

וְאֶת־לַחֲצֵנוּ · זֶה הַדֹּחַק · כְּמָה שֶׁנֶּאֱמַר : וְגַם־רָאִיתִי אֶת־הַלַּחַץ אֲשֶׁר מִצְרַיִם לֹחֲצִים אֹתָם :

And the Lord brought us out of Egypt with a mighty hand and with an outstretched arm and with great terror and with signs and with wonders. (Deut. xxvi. 8)

וַיּוֹצִאֵנוּ יְיָ מִמִּצְרַיִם בְּיָד חֲזָקָה וּבִזְרֹעַ נְטוּיָה וּבְמֹרָא גָּדֹל · וּבְאֹתוֹת וּבְמֹפְתִים :

And the Lord brought us out of Egypt — not by the hand of an angel, and not by the hand of a seraph, and not by the hand of a messenger, but the Holy One, blessed be He, in His glory and in His person, as it is said: 'For I will go through the land of Egypt in that night, and I will smite all the first-born in the land of Egypt, both man and beast, and against all the gods of Egypt will I execute judgement: I am the Lord.' (Ex. xii. 12)

וַיּוֹצִאֵנוּ יְיָ מִמִּצְרַיִם · לֹא־עַל־יְדֵי מַלְאָךְ · וְלֹא־עַל־יְדֵי שָׂרָף · וְלֹא־עַל־יְדֵי שָׁלִיחַ · אֶלָּא הַקָּדוֹשׁ בָּרוּךְ הוּא בִּכְבוֹדוֹ וּבְעַצְמוֹ · שֶׁנֶּאֱמַר : וְעָבַרְתִּי בְאֶרֶץ־מִצְרַיִם בַּלַּיְלָה הַזֶּה · וְהִכֵּיתִי כָל־בְּכוֹר בְּאֶרֶץ מִצְרַיִם מֵאָדָם וְעַד־בְּהֵמָה · וּבְכָל־אֱלֹהֵי מִצְרַיִם אֶעֱשֶׂה שְׁפָטִים אֲנִי יְיָ :

For I will go through the land of Egypt in that night — I, not an angel: *And I will smite all*

וְעָבַרְתִּי בְאֶרֶץ־מִצְרַיִם בַּלַּיְלָה הַזֶּה · אֲנִי וְלֹא מַלְאָךְ ·

24

the *first-born in the land of Egypt* — I, not a seraph: *And against all the gods of Egypt will I execute judgement* — I, not a messenger. *I am the Lord* — I am he, and no other.

וְהִכֵּיתִי כָל־בְּכוֹר בְּאֶרֶץ מִצְרַיִם. אֲנִי וְלֹא שָׂרָף · וּבְכָל־ אֱלֹהֵי מִצְרַיִם אֶעֱשֶׂה שְׁפָטִים · אֲנִי וְלֹא שָׁלִיחַ · אֲנִי יְיָ. אֲנִי הוּא וְלֹא אַחֵר :

D. NACHSHEN

With a mighty hand: this refers to the murrain, as it is said, 'Behold, the *hand* of the Lord is upon thy cattle which is in the field, upon the horses, upon the asses, upon the

בְּיָד חֲזָקָה · זוֹ הַדֶּבֶר · כְּמָה שֶׁנֶּאֱמַר: הִנֵּה יַד־יְיָ הוֹיָה בְּמִקְנְךָ אֲשֶׁר בַּשָּׂדֶה בַּסּוּסִים

camels, upon the herds, and upon the flocks; there shall be a very grievous murrain.' (Ex. ix. 3)

בַּחֲמֹרִים בַּגְּמַלִּים בַּבָּקָר וּבַצֹּאן· דֶּבֶר כָּבֵד מְאֹד:

And with an outstretched arm: this refers to the sword, as it is said, 'And a drawn sword in his hand *outstretched* over Jerusalem.' (I Chron. xxi. 16)

וּבִזְרֹעַ נְטוּיָה· זוֹ הַחֶרֶב. כְּמָה שֶׁנֶּאֱמַר· וְחַרְבּוֹ שְׁלוּפָה בְּיָדוֹ נְטוּיָה עַל־יְרוּשָׁלַיִם:

And with great terror: this refers to the manifestation of the Divine Presence, as it is said: 'Or hath God essayed to go and take him a nation from the midst of another nation by temptations, by signs, and by wonders, and by war, and by a mighty hand, and by an outstretched arm and by *great terrors*, according to all that the Lord your God did for you in Egypt before your eyes?' (Deut. iv. 34)

וּבְמֹרָא גָּדֹל· זוֹ גִּלּוּי שְׁכִינָה, כְּמָה שֶׁנֶּאֱמַר: אוֹ הֲנִסָּה אֱלֹהִים לָבוֹא לָקַחַת לוֹ גוֹי מִקֶּרֶב גּוֹי בְּמַסֹּת בְּאֹתֹת וּבְמוֹפְתִים וּבְמִלְחָמָה וּבְיָד חֲזָקָה וּבִזְרֹעַ נְטוּיָה וּבְמוֹרָאִים גְּדֹלִים· כְּכֹל אֲשֶׁר־עָשָׂה לָכֶם יְיָ אֱלֹהֵיכֶם בְּמִצְרַיִם לְעֵינֶיךָ:

And with signs: this refers to the Rod, as it is said: 'And thou shalt take in thy hand this rod, wherewith thou shalt do the *signs.*' (Ex. iv. 17)

וּבְאֹתוֹת· זֶה הַמַּטֶּה· כְּמָה שֶׁנֶּאֱמַר: וְאֶת־הַמַּטֶּה הַזֶּה תִּקַּח בְּיָדֶךָ· אֲשֶׁר תַּעֲשֶׂה־בּוֹ אֶת־הָאֹתֹת:

And with wonders: this refers to the blood, as it is said: 'And I will shew *wonders* in the heavens and in the earth: blood, and fire, and pillars of smoke.' (Joel ii. 30)

וּבְמוֹפְתִים· זֶה הַדָּם· כְּמָה שֶׁנֶּאֱמַר: וְנָתַתִּי מוֹפְתִים בַּשָּׁמַיִם וּבָאָרֶץ· דָּם וָאֵשׁ וְתִמְרוֹת עָשָׁן:

26

Another explanation is as follows: 'with a *strong hand*' indicates two: 'and with an *outstretched arm*', two: 'and with *great terror*', two: 'and with *signs*', two: 'and with *wonders*' two.

דָּבָר אַחֵר . בְּיָד חֲזָקָה שְׁתַּיִם . וּבִזְרֹעַ נְטוּיָה שְׁתַּיִם . וּבְמֹרָא גָּדֹל שְׁתַּיִם . וּבְאֹתוֹת שְׁתַּיִם . וּבְמֹפְתִים שְׁתַּיִם :

This indicates the Ten Blows which the Holy One, blessed be He, brought upon the Egyptians in Egypt, to wit:

אֵלּוּ עֶשֶׂר מַכּוֹת שֶׁהֵבִיא הַקָּדוֹשׁ בָּרוּךְ הוּא עַל־הַמִּצְרִים בְּמִצְרַיִם . וְאֵלּוּ הֵן :

BLOOD   FROGS   LICE
BEASTS   MURRAIN
BOILS   HAIL
LOCUSTS   DARKNESS
SLAYING OF THE FIRST-BORN

דָּם . צְפַרְדֵּעַ . כִּנִּים . עָרוֹב . דֶּבֶר . שְׁחִין . בָּרָד . אַרְבֶּה . חֹשֶׁךְ . מַכַּת־בְּכוֹרוֹת :

Rabbi Judah used to refer to them by abbreviation, thus:

רַבִּי יְהוּדָה הָיָה נוֹתֵן בָּהֶם סִמָּנִים .

דְּצַ"ךְ . עֲדַ"שׁ . בְּאַחַ"ב :

THE TEN PLAGUES: The connection of the Ten Plagues (or, more accurately, the Ten Blows) with the *Seder* Service is obvious: and they have given great opportunities to the fantasy of the various generations of illustrators. There is an ancient custom of spilling a little wine from the goblet, or sprinkling a little of it with the finger, at the mention of each one of them: no doubt, in origin a deliberate waste intended to avert ill-fortune by providing a safeguard against immoderate and unmitigated rejoicing. It is a curious practice, which finds interesting parallels in general folk-lore.

BEASTS: The fourth plague, according to the Jewish tradition, consisted of ravening wild beasts: according to the Anglican versions and modern authorities, of flies.

THE ABREVIATIONS AND AMPLIFICATIONS: The abbreviation here given (which, according to him, was inscribed on the wonder-working rod of Moses) was devised by Rabbi Judah bar Ammi, a Palestinian scholar of the fourth century, and is formed of the initial letters of each of the Plagues. It is intended to make the sequence more easily remembered, as well as to prevent words of ill-omen from crossing the lips in full. The mnemonic has been distorted into an ingenious semblance of a meaning: 'The scorpion stung the uncle'. Following this we have a reversal of this tendency, the exaggeration instead of the diminution of the disasters. It must not be thought, however, that this breathes a spirit of vengefulness. The idea of the Rabbis (Jose the Galilæan, Eleazar son of Hyrcanus, and Akiba — all contemporary figures, of the second century) was to magnify the achievements of the Lord, not to gloat over the punishment of His foes. Such an attitude would have been far removed from the Jewish ideal, which deprecated all suffering. There is a significant Rabbinical legend relating to the Passover period which brings this out to the full. God is represented as saying, reproachfully, to His angels, who joined in the song of jubilation chanted by the Israelites upon the overthrow of their enemies in the Red Sea: 'What! the works of My hands are sunk in the waters, yet ye can sing songs before Me!' There is a restraint in the liturgy on the last days of Passover which reflects the Rabbinic

27

Rabbi Jose, the Galilæan, said: Whence canst thou deduce that, if the Egyptians were smitten with ten blows in Egypt, then upon the sea they were smitten with fifty blows? With regard to Egypt, what does the text say? 'Then the magicians said unto Pharaoh, This is the *finger* of God' (Ex. VIII. 15): and at the sea, what does the text say? 'And Israel saw the great *hand* which the Lord laid upon the Egyptians: and the people feared the Lord, and they believed in the Lord, and in His servant Moses.' (Ex. XIV. 31) How many were they smitten by the *finger*? Ten blows. Deduce hence that in Egypt they were smitten with ten blows, while at the sea they were smitten with fifty blows.

Rabbi Eliezer said: Whence may it be deduced that every blow which the Holy One, blessed be He, brought upon the Egyptians in Egypt was equivalent to four blows? It is said: 'He cast upon them the fierceness of His anger, wrath, and indignation, and trouble, a band of angels of evil.' (Ps. LXXVIII. 49) 'Wrath' indicates one: 'indignation', two: 'trouble', three: 'a band of angels of evil', four. Deduce hence that in Egypt they were smitten with forty blows, while at the sea they were afflicted with two hundred blows.

Rabbi Akiba said: Whence may it be deduced that every blow which the Holy One, blessed be He, brought upon the Egyptians in Egypt was equivalent to five blows? It is written: 'He cast upon them the fierceness of His anger, wrath,

רַבִּי יוֹסֵי הַגְּלִילִי אוֹמֵר . מִנַּיִן אַתָּה אוֹמֵר שֶׁלָּקוּ הַמִּצְרִים בְּמִצְרַיִם עֶשֶׂר מַכּוֹת . וְעַל־הַיָּם לָקוּ חֲמִשִּׁים מַכּוֹת: בְּמִצְרַיִם מַה־הוּא אוֹמֵר . וַיֹּאמְרוּ הַחַרְטֻמִּים אֶל־ פַּרְעֹה אֶצְבַּע אֱלֹהִים הִוא . וְעַל־הַיָּם מַה־ הוּא אוֹמֵר . וַיַּרְא יִשְׂרָאֵל אֶת־הַיָּד הַגְּדֹלָה אֲשֶׁר עָשָׂה יְיָ בְּמִצְרַיִם וַיִּירְאוּ הָעָם אֶת־יְיָ וַיַּאֲמִינוּ בַּיְיָ וּבְמֹשֶׁה עַבְדּוֹ: כַּמָּה לָקוּ בָאֶצְבַּע . עֶשֶׂר מַכּוֹת . אֱמוֹר מֵעַתָּה בְּמִצְרַיִם לָקוּ עֶשֶׂר מַכּוֹת וְעַל־הַיָּם לָקוּ חֲמִשִּׁים מַכּוֹת :

רַבִּי אֱלִיעֶזֶר אוֹמֵר . מִנַּיִן שֶׁכָּל־מַכָּה וּמַכָּה שֶׁהֵבִיא הַקָּדוֹשׁ בָּרוּךְ הוּא עַל־ הַמִּצְרִים בְּמִצְרַיִם הָיְתָה שֶׁל אַרְבַּע מַכּוֹת . שֶׁנֶּאֱמַר: יְשַׁלַּח־בָּם חֲרוֹן אַפּוֹ עֶבְרָה וָזַעַם וְצָרָה מִשְׁלַחַת מַלְאֲכֵי רָעִים: עֶבְרָה אֶחָת . וָזַעַם שְׁתַּיִם . וְצָרָה שָׁלֹשׁ . מִשְׁלַחַת מַלְאֲכֵי רָעִים אַרְבַּע : אֱמוֹר מֵעַתָּה . בְּמִצְרַיִם לָקוּ אַרְבָּעִים מַכּוֹת וְעַל־הַיָּם לָקוּ מָאתַיִם מַכּוֹת :

רַבִּי עֲקִיבָא אוֹמֵר . מִנַּיִן שֶׁכָּל־מַכָּה וּמַכָּה שֶׁהֵבִיא הַקָּדוֹשׁ בָּרוּךְ הוּא עַל־ הַמִּצְרִים בְּמִצְרַיִם הָיְתָה שֶׁל חָמֵשׁ מַכּוֹת . שֶׁנֶּאֱמַר: יְשַׁלַּח־בָּם חֲרוֹן אַפּוֹ עֶבְרָה וָזַעַם

view, that there must be some qualification of the festive feeling on a day marked by such a disaster to a branch of the human race. From scholars with so delicate and so universal a sense of humanity, a purely vindictive piece of exegesis such as is commonly imagined at this point is not to be suspected. The source of the passage is in various ancient *Midrashim* (Mekhilta to Exodus, vi: Tanhuma to Exodus vii, 1: Midrash Tehillim, Psalm lxxv).

and indignation, and trouble, a band of angels of evil.' (*Ibid.*) 'The fierceness of His anger' indicates one: 'wrath', two: 'indignation', three: 'trouble', four: 'a band of angels of evil', five. Deduce hence that in Egypt they were smitten with fifty blows, while at the sea they were smitten with two hundred and fifty blows.

וְצָרָה מִשְׁלַחַת מַלְאֲכֵי רָעִים: חֲרוֹן אַפּוֹ אַחַת. עֶבְרָה שְׁתַּיִם. וָזַעַם שָׁלשׁ. וְצָרָה אַרְבַּע. מִשְׁלַחַת מַלְאֲכֵי רָעִים חָמֵשׁ: אֱמוֹר מֵעַתָּה. בְּמִצְרַיִם לָקוּ חֲמִשִּׁים מַכּוֹת וְעַל־ הַיָּם לָקוּ חֲמִשִּׁים וּמָאתַיִם מַכּוֹת:

How many are the calls of the Almighty upon our thankfulness!

כַּמָּה מַעֲלוֹת טוֹבוֹת לַמָּקוֹם עָלֵינוּ:

Had He brought us out of Egypt,
    And not executed judgement on them
        It had sufficed us!

אִלּוּ הוֹצִיאָנוּ מִמִּצְרַיִם. וְלֹא עָשָׂה בָהֶם שְׁפָטִים· דַּיֵּנוּ:

IT HAD SUFFICED US: The elaboration of the story of the Exodus which has just been read leads up to a hymn of thanksgiving — the first of those which occur in the *Seder* Service. The significance is simple enough — that the deliverance from Egypt was in itself ample ground for the gratitude which should be felt towards God, the subsequent manifestations of the Divine providence heightening the debt more and more. The idea is taken from the Sifre to Deuteronomy, cap. xxxii, but the exact authorship of the hymn is unknown. It is, however, a specimen of the Hebrew liturgical poem in its most primitive form, and probably dates back to the sixth or seventh century. It is noteworthy, however, that it was omitted by Maimonides in his formulary of the *Haggadah*.

One passage in the poem calls for comment. The fourth stanza speaks of the 'despoiling' of the Egyptians by the children of Israel, as mentioned in Exodus (xii. 35). It is one of the passages which usually forms the object of spiteful sneering: The children of Israel, we are told, 'borrowed' from the Egyptians, who 'lent' them what they asked. But this libel is based on a mistranslation. The Hebrew text undoubtedly means that they asked, as a gift, whatever they fancied, everything being given to them freely. All the modern versions concur without question in this rendering, which puts so different a light upon the whole matter.

As a matter of fact, one is struck in this poem by the sheer immateriality of most of the favours indicated. Through its crude phraseology and primitive execution one catches a glimpse of that typical Rabbinical idea, that the work of the Redemption from Egypt was not completed until the *Torah* had been promulgated and settled religious worship established in Israel's own land. It is this which serves as the climax.

29

Had He executed judgement on them,
But not wrought justice on their gods
It had sufficed us!

אִלּוּ עָשָׂה בָהֶם שְׁפָטִים.
וְלֹא עָשָׂה דִין בֵּאלֹהֵיהֶם.
דַּיֵּנוּ:

Had He wrought justice on their gods,
And not slain their first-born
It had sufficed us!

אִלּוּ עָשָׂה דִין בֵּאלֹהֵיהֶם.
וְלֹא הָרַג בְּכוֹרֵיהֶם. דַּיֵּנוּ:

Had He slain their first-born,
And not given us their substance
It had sufficed us!

אִלּוּ הָרַג בְּכוֹרֵיהֶם.
וְלֹא נָתַן לָנוּ אֶת־מָמוֹנָם.
דַּיֵּנוּ:

Had He given us their substance,
And not cleft us the sea
It had sufficed us!

אִלּוּ נָתַן לָנוּ אֶת־מָמוֹנָם.
וְלֹא קָרַע לָנוּ אֶת־הַיָּם.
דַּיֵּנוּ:

Had He cleft us the sea,
And not brought us through it dryshod
It had sufficed us!

אִלּוּ קָרַע לָנוּ אֶת־הַיָּם.
וְלֹא הֶעֱבִירָנוּ בְּתוֹכוֹ
בֶּחָרָבָה. דַּיֵּנוּ:

Had He brought us through it dryshod,
And not sunk our oppressors in its depths
It had sufficed us!

אִלּוּ הֶעֱבִירָנוּ בְּתוֹכוֹ בֶּחָרָבָה.
וְלֹא שִׁקַּע צָרֵינוּ בְּתוֹכוֹ.
דַּיֵּנוּ:

Had He sunk our oppressors
in its depths,
   And not satisfied our wants
   in the wilderness for forty
   years
         It had sufficed us!

אִלּוּ שִׁקַּע צָרֵינוּ בְּתוֹכוֹ.

וְלֹא סִפֵּק צָרְכֵּינוּ בַּמִּדְבָּר

אַרְבָּעִים שָׁנָה.   דַּיֵּנוּ:

Had He satisfied our wants
in the wilderness for forty
years,
   And not fed us with the
   manna
        It had sufficed us!

אִלּוּ סִפֵּק צָרְכֵּינוּ בַּמִּדְבָּר

אַרְבָּעִים שָׁנָה.

וְלֹא הֶאֱכִילָנוּ אֶת־הַמָּן.

דַּיֵּנוּ:

31

Had He fed us with the manna,
    And not given us the Sabbath
        It had sufficed us!

אִלּוּ הֶאֱכִילָנוּ אֶת־הַמָּן.
וְלֹא נָתַן לָנוּ אֶת־הַשַּׁבָּת.
דַּיֵּנוּ:

Had He given us the Sabbath,
    And not brought us to the Mount of Sinai
        It had sufficed us!

אִלּוּ נָתַן לָנוּ אֶת־הַשַּׁבָּת.
וְלֹא קֵרְבָנוּ לִפְנֵי הַר סִינָי.
דַּיֵּנוּ:

Had He brought us to the Mount of Sinai,
    And not given us the Law
        It had sufficed us!

אִלּוּ קֵרְבָנוּ לִפְנֵי הַר סִינָי.
וְלֹא נָתַן לָנוּ אֶת־הַתּוֹרָה.
דַּיֵּנוּ:

Had He given us the Law,
    And not brought us into the Land of Israel
        It had sufficed us!

אִלּוּ נָתַן לָנוּ אֶת־הַתּוֹרָה.
וְלֹא הִכְנִיסָנוּ לְאֶרֶץ יִשְׂרָאֵל.
דַּיֵּנוּ:

Had He brought us into the Land of Israel,
    And not built us the Chosen Temple
        It had sufficed us!

אִלּוּ הִכְנִיסָנוּ לְאֶרֶץ יִשְׂרָאֵל.
וְלֹא בָנָה לָנוּ אֶת־בֵּית
הַבְּחִירָה.
דַּיֵּנוּ:

f

How much more so, then, hath the Almighty a double, and redoubled, call upon our thankfulness! For He brought us out of Egypt, and executed judgement on them, and wrought justice on their gods, and slew their first-born, and gave us their substance, and cleft us the sea, and brought us through it dry-shod, and sank our oppressors in its depths, and satisfied our wants in the wilderness for forty years, and fed us with the manna, and gave us the Sabbath, and brought us to the Mount of Sinai, and gave us the Law, and brought us into the land of Israel and built us the chosen Temple to atone for all our sins.

עַל־אַחַת כַּמָּה וְכַמָּה טוֹבָה כְפוּלָה וּמְכֻפֶּלֶת לַמָּקוֹם עָלֵינוּ. שֶׁהוֹצִיאָנוּ מִמִּצְרַיִם. וְעָשָׂה בָהֶם שְׁפָטִים. וְעָשָׂה דִין בֵּאלֹהֵיהֶם. וְהָרַג בְּכוֹרֵיהֶם. וְנָתַן לָנוּ אֶת־מָמוֹנָם. וְקָרַע לָנוּ אֶת־הַיָּם. וְהֶעֱבִירָנוּ בְתוֹכוֹ בֶּחָרָבָה. וְשִׁקַּע צָרֵינוּ בְּתוֹכוֹ. וְסִפֵּק צָרְכֵּנוּ בַּמִּדְבָּר אַרְבָּעִים שָׁנָה. וְהֶאֱכִילָנוּ אֶת־הַמָּן. וְנָתַן לָנוּ אֶת־הַשַּׁבָּת. וְקֵרְבָנוּ לִפְנֵי הַר סִינַי. וְנָתַן לָנוּ אֶת־הַתּוֹרָה. וְהִכְנִיסָנוּ לְאֶרֶץ יִשְׂרָאֵל. וּבָנָה לָנוּ אֶת־בֵּית הַבְּחִירָה. לְכַפֵּר עַל־כָּל־עֲוֹנוֹתֵינוּ:

Rabban Gamaliel said: Any person who does not make mention of the following three things on Passover has not fulfilled his obligation; and these are they:

רַבָּן גַּמְלִיאֵל אוֹמֵר: כָּל־שֶׁלֹּא אָמַר שְׁלֹשָׁה דְבָרִים אֵלּוּ בַּפֶּסַח לֹא יָצָא יְדֵי חוֹבָתוֹ: וְאֵלּוּ הֵן:

the Passover,

פֶּסַח.

the Unleavened Bread,

מַצָּה.

and the Bitter Herb.

וּמָרוֹר:

RABBAN GAMALIEL SAID: This statement, with what follows, is an almost literal quotation from the *Mishnah*, Pesahim x. 5, with an unimportant addition recommended in the *Gemara* in its commentary to that passage. The author is Rabban Gamaliel, the Patriarch (died *c.* 95) — an aristocratic figure, grandson of the pious Hillel, and grandfather of Rabbi Judah the Prince. Members of this family, in which the names of Hillel, Judah and Gamaliel continued to alternate, functioned uninterruptedly as the Patriarchs of Palestinian Jewry, down to the abolition of the office in the fifth century.

33

The Passover which our fathers used to eat at the time when the Temple was standing — because of what is it? It is because the Holy One, Blessed **be He**, passed over the houses of our fathers in Egypt, as it is said: 'And ye shall say, It is the sacrifice of the Lord's Passover, for that he passed over the houses of the children of Israel in Egypt, when he smote the Egyptians, and delivered our houses. And the people bowed the head, and worshipped.' (Ex. xii. 27)

פֶּסַח שֶׁהָיוּ אֲבוֹתֵינוּ אוֹכְלִים בִּזְמַן שֶׁבֵּית הַמִּקְדָּשׁ הָיָה קַיָּם עַל־שׁוּם מָה. עַל־שׁוּם שֶׁפָּסַח הַקָּדוֹשׁ בָּרוּךְ הוּא עַל־בָּתֵּי אֲבוֹתֵינוּ בְּמִצְרַיִם. שֶׁנֶּאֱמַר: וַאֲמַרְתֶּם זֶבַח־פֶּסַח הוּא לַיָי אֲשֶׁר פָּסַח עַל־בָּתֵּי בְנֵי־יִשְׂרָאֵל בְּמִצְרַיִם בְּנָגְפּוֹ אֶת־מִצְרַיִם וְאֶת־בָּתֵּינוּ הִצִּיל. וַיִּקֹּד הָעָם וַיִּשְׁתַּחֲווּ:

The Celebrant points to the Mazzah:

This Unleavened Bread which we eat — because of what is it? It is because there was no time for the dough of our fathers to become leavened before the supreme King of Kings, the Holy One, Blessed be He, revealed himself unto them and redeemed them, as it is said: 'And they baked un-

מַצָּה זוּ שֶׁאָנוּ אוֹכְלִים עַל־שׁוּם מָה. עַל־שׁוּם שֶׁלֹּא הִסְפִּיק בְּצֵקָם שֶׁל־אֲבוֹתֵינוּ לְהַחֲמִיץ עַד־שֶׁנִּגְלָה עֲלֵיהֶם מֶלֶךְ מַלְכֵי הַמְּלָכִים הַקָּדוֹשׁ בָּרוּךְ הוּא וּגְאָלָם: שֶׁנֶּאֱמַר: וַיֹּאפוּ אֶת־הַבָּצֵק אֲשֶׁר הוֹצִיאוּ

34

leavened cakes of the dough which they brought forth out of Egypt, for it was not leavened: because they were thrust out of Egypt, and could not tarry, neither had they prepared for themselves any victual.' (Ex. xii. 39)

מִמִּצְרַיִם עֻגֹת מַצּוֹת כִּי לֹא חָמֵץ ּ כִּי־גֹרְשׁוּ מִמִּצְרַיִם וְלֹא יָכְלוּ לְהִתְמַהְמֵהַּ וְגַם־צֵדָה לֹא־עָשׂוּ לָהֶם׃

The Celebrant points to the Bitter Herb:

This Bitter Herb which we eat — because of what is it? It is because the Egyptians embittered the lives of our fathers in Egypt, as it is written: 'And they made their lives bitter with hard bondage, in morter and in brick, and in all manner of service in the field: all their service wherein they made them serve, was with rigour.' (Ex. i. 14)

מָרוֹר זֶה שֶׁאָנוּ אוֹכְלִים עַל־שׁוּם מָה ּ עַל־שׁוּם שֶׁמֵּרְרוּ הַמִּצְרִים אֶת־חַיֵּי אֲבוֹתֵינוּ בְּמִצְרַיִם ּ שֶׁנֶּאֱמַר ּ וַיְמָרְרוּ אֶת־חַיֵּיהֶם בַּעֲבֹדָה קָשָׁה בְּחֹמֶר וּבִלְבֵנִים וּבְכָל־עֲבֹדָה בַּשָּׂדֶה ּ אֵת כָּל־עֲבֹדָתָם אֲשֶׁר־עָבְדוּ בָהֶם בְּפָרֶךְ׃

It is customary for the *Mazzah* and the bitter herb to be raised up, or else pointed out, as their significance is described. This is not, however, the case with the shankbone, which is only a symbol of the Paschal sacrifice, not the reality. Any semblance of imitating this was therefore carefully avoided. Already in the second century a communal leader in Rome, named Theudas, was prevented by some visiting Palestinian scholars from permitting the community (already at that time of considerable numerical importance) to feast off roast lamb, in imitation of the Temple usage, on the Passover eve. It is customary indeed in many places, so as to forestall any possibility of misinterpretation, to abstain from meat entirely during the *Seder* meal.

Mention has already been made of the old witticism, which has received pictorial status in some *Haggadahs*, whereby the Celebrant points to his wife on mentioning the Bitter Herb. Is there any other race, one wonders, which can introduce the element of humour even into its religious rites?

35

In every single generation is
it a man's duty to regard
himself as if he had gone
forth from Egypt, as it is
written: 'And thou shalt shew
thy son in that day, saying,
Because of that which the
Lord did unto *me* when I
came forth out of Egypt'.
(Ex. xiii. 8) Not our fathers only
did the Holy One, Blessed be
He, redeem, but us also He
redeemed with them; as it is
said: 'And he brought *us* out
from thence, that he might
bring us in, to give us the
land which he sware unto
our fathers'. (Deut. vi. 23)

בְּכָל־דּוֹר וָדוֹר חַיָּב אָדָם
לִרְאוֹת אֶת־עַצְמוֹ כְּאִלּוּ הוּא
יָצָא מִמִּצְרַיִם· שֶׁנֶּאֱמַר· וְהִגַּדְתָּ
לְבִנְךָ בַּיּוֹם הַהוּא לֵאמֹר·
בַּעֲבוּר זֶה עָשָׂה יְיָ לִי בְּצֵאתִי
מִמִּצְרָיִם: לֹא אֶת־אֲבוֹתֵינוּ
בִּלְבַד גָּאַל הַקָּדוֹשׁ בָּרוּךְ הוּא·
אֶלָּא אַף אוֹתָנוּ גָּאַל עִמָּהֶם·
שֶׁנֶּאֱמַר· וְאוֹתָנוּ הוֹצִיא מִשָּׁם·
לְמַעַן הָבִיא אוֹתָנוּ לָתֶת לָנוּ
אֶת־הָאָרֶץ אֲשֶׁר נִשְׁבַּע
לַאֲבֹתֵינוּ:

Here the cup is raised:

It is therefore our duty to
thank, praise, laud, glorify,
exalt, honour, bless, extol,
and adore Him who per-
formed for our fathers and
for us all of these wonders.

לְפִיכָךְ אֲנַחְנוּ חַיָּבִים לְהוֹדוֹת·
לְהַלֵּל· לְשַׁבֵּחַ· לְפָאֵר· לְרוֹמֵם·
לְהַדֵּר· לְבָרֵךְ· לְעַלֵּה· וּלְקַלֵּס·
לְמִי שֶׁעָשָׂה לַאֲבוֹתֵינוּ וְלָנוּ

IT IS THEREFORE OUR DUTY: In this noble passage, the ritual of the evening reaches its climax.
It leads up naturally to the recital of the Festal Psalms, or *Hallel*, with which the first half of
the service concludes. The source of the passage is in the *Mishnah*, in the same place as the
preceding paragraphs.

He brought us forth from slavery to freedom, from anguish to joy, from mourning to holy-day, from darkness to great light, and from bondage to redemption. Let us sing, therefore, before Him a new song. Hallelujah!

אֶת־כָּל־הַנִּסִּים הָאֵלּוּ. הוֹצִיאָנוּ מֵעַבְדוּת לְחֵרוּת. מִיָּגוֹן לְשִׂמְחָה. וּמֵאֵבֶל לְיוֹם טוֹב. וּמֵאֲפֵלָה לְאוֹר גָּדוֹל. וּמִשִּׁעְבּוּד לִגְאֻלָּה. וְנֹאמַר לְפָנָיו שִׁירָה חֲדָשָׁה הַלְלוּיָה:

HALLELUJAH: The conventional transliteration of the familiar Hebrew term, which is more than naturalised in English, is used here, as it seems to serve as a synonym of the 'new song' referred to in the text. The literal translation is, of course, 'Praise ye the Lord', as it is rendered immediately after.

PRAISE YE THE LORD

הַלְלוּיָהּ

Praise, O ye servants of the Lord, praise the Name of the Lord. Let the Name of the Lord be blessed from this time forth and for evermore. From the rising of the sun until the going down thereof the Lord's Name is to be praised. The Lord is high above all nations, and His glory above the heavens. Who is like unto the Lord our God, that dwelleth so high; that looketh down so

הַלְלוּ עַבְדֵי יְיָ. הַלְלוּ אֶת־שֵׁם
יְיָ: יְהִי שֵׁם יְיָ מְבֹרָךְ מֵעַתָּה
וְעַד־עוֹלָם: מִמִּזְרַח־שֶׁמֶשׁ עַד־
מְבוֹאוֹ מְהֻלָּל שֵׁם יְיָ: רָם עַל־
כָּל־גּוֹיִם יְיָ עַל־הַשָּׁמַיִם כְּבוֹדוֹ:
מִי כַּיְיָ אֱלֹהֵינוּ הַמַּגְבִּיהִי
לָשָׁבֶת: הַמַּשְׁפִּילִי לִרְאוֹת
בַּשָּׁמַיִם וּבָאָרֶץ: מְקִימִי מֵעָפָר

THE HALLEL: The *Hallel*, or 'Praise' *par excellence*, is the name given in the Jewish liturgy to the glorious sequence of Psalms, cxiii to cxviii, recited on all festive occasions. More fully, the title is 'The Egyptian *Hallel*', owing to the special prominence given in Psalm cxiv (the famous '*In Exitu Israel*' of the Catholic Church and Dante) to the Exodus. According to Rabbinic fancy, indeed, these psalms were first sung by the children of Israel at the passage of the Red Sea — a legend which would account still further for the title. This was used in contradistinction to 'The Great *Hallel*', the title applied to Psalm cxxxvi, which is recited later on. The Egyptian *Hallel* used to be chanted by the Levites in the Temple while the Paschal offering was being sacrificed: and it is here introduced for that reason. Only the first two of the psalms comprised in it, leading up more specifically to the Exodus, are recited at this stage: the rest, more typically hymnal, follow after the meal. The apparent references in the sequence to a hard-fought war crowned with ultimate success, coupled with linguistic evidence, make modern critics inclined to assign the composition to the period of the Maccabees.

low upon the heavens and earth! He raiseth up the lowly out of the dust, and lifteth up the needy from the dung-hill; that He may set him with princes, even with the princes of His people. He maketh the barren woman to dwell in her house as a joyful mother of children. Praise ye the Lord.

דָּל מֵאַשְׁפֹּת יָרִים אֶבְיוֹן: לְהוֹשִׁיבִי עִם־נְדִיבִים עִם נְדִיבֵי עַמּוֹ: מוֹשִׁיבִי עֲקֶרֶת הַבַּיִת אֵם־הַבָּנִים שְׂמֵחָה הַלְלוּיָהּ:

PSALM CXIV. When Israel went forth out of Egypt, the house of Jacob from a people of strange language; Judah became his sanctuary, Israel his dominion. The sea saw it, and fled; Jordan turned back. The mountains skipped like rams, the hills like lambs. What aileth thee, O thou sea, that thou fleest? Thou Jordan, that thou turnest back? Ye mountains that ye skip like rams? Ye hills, like lambs? At the presence of the Lord tremble, O earth, at the presence of the God of Jacob; who turned the rock into a pool of water, the flint into a fountain of waters.

בְּצֵאת יִשְׂרָאֵל מִמִּצְרָיִם בֵּית יַעֲקֹב מֵעַם לֹעֵז: הָיְתָה יְהוּדָה לְקָדְשׁוֹ יִשְׂרָאֵל מַמְשְׁלוֹתָיו: הַיָּם רָאָה וַיָּנֹס הַיַּרְדֵּן יִסֹּב לְאָחוֹר: הֶהָרִים רָקְדוּ כְאֵילִים גְּבָעוֹת כִּבְנֵי־צֹאן: מַה־לְּךָ הַיָּם כִּי תָנוּס הַיַּרְדֵּן תִּסֹּב לְאָחוֹר: הֶהָרִים תִּרְקְדוּ כְאֵילִים גְּבָעוֹת כִּבְנֵי־צֹאן: מִלִּפְנֵי אָדוֹן חוּלִי אָרֶץ מִלִּפְנֵי אֱלוֹהַּ יַעֲקֹב: הַהֹפְכִי הַצּוּר אֲגַם־מָיִם חַלָּמִישׁ לְמַעְיְנוֹ־מָיִם:

Blessed art Thou, O Lord, King of the Universe, who redeemed us, and redeemed our Fathers, from Egypt, and enabled us to reach this night, whereon to eat unleavened bread and bitter herb. Likewise, O Lord our God and God of our Fathers, do Thou enable us to reach other an-niversaries and feasts (may they come to us in peace!), joyous in the building of Thy

בָּרוּךְ אַתָּה יְיָ אֱלֹהֵינוּ מֶלֶךְ הָעוֹלָם. אֲשֶׁר גְּאָלָנוּ וְגָאַל אֶת־אֲבוֹתֵינוּ מִמִּצְרַיִם וְהִגִּיעָנוּ הַלַּיְלָה הַזֶּה לֶאֱכָל־בּוֹ מַצָּה וּמָרוֹר. כֵּן יְיָ אֱלֹהֵינוּ וֵאלֹהֵי אֲבוֹתֵינוּ הַגִּיעֵנוּ לְמוֹעֲדִים וְלִרְגָלִים אֲחֵרִים הַבָּאִים לִקְרָאתֵנוּ לְשָׁלוֹם שְׂמֵחִים

39

city and exultant in Thy service. There shall we partake of the sacrifices and of the Paschal offerings the blood of which shall be acceptably sprinkled upon the wall of Thy altar: and there shall we chant unto Thee a New Song, for our redemption and for the salvation of our beings. Blessed art Thou, O Lord, who redeemed Israel!

Blessed art Thou, O Lord, our God, King of the Universe, Creator of the fruit of the vine.

בְּבִנְיַן עִירֶךָ וְשָׂשִׂים בַּעֲבוֹדָתֶךָ. וְנֹאכַל שָׁם מִן הַזְּבָחִים וּמִן הַפְּסָחִים אֲשֶׁר יַגִּיעַ דָּמָם עַל־קִיר מִזְבַּחֲךָ לְרָצוֹן. וְנוֹדֶה לְךָ שִׁיר חָדָשׁ עַל־גְּאֻלָּתֵנוּ וְעַל פְּדוּת נַפְשֵׁנוּ: בָּרוּךְ אַתָּה יְיָ. גָּאַל יִשְׂרָאֵל:

בָּרוּךְ אַתָּה יְיָ אֱלֹהֵינוּ מֶלֶךְ הָעוֹלָם. בּוֹרֵא פְּרִי הַגָּפֶן:

The second cup of wine is here drunk.

THE CONCLUDING BLESSING: This benedictory formula (the Blessing of Redemption) sets the seal upon the *Hallel* and serves to conclude the first part of the *Haggadah*. Its source is in the *Mishnah*, Pesahim x. 6. Rabbi Tarphon, a dry legalist (whom we have met above), prescribed that one should say: 'Who hath redeemed us, and redeemed our Fathers, from Egypt' a sober historical reference to what had happened. Rabbi Akiba, that enthusiastic patriot (rightly mentioned in the *Haggadah* more frequently than any other scholar), was not content with this form. He regarded the Passover as a type of the Redemption that was to come in the future. Accordingly, he added to this a prayer for the restoration of the Temple to its ancient glories and for the hastening of the time when the Passover would be observed once more according to all of its due rites and ceremonies, in the Place which God had chosen. It is this more optimistic formula which the ritual at present preserves.

The masculine form of the word for song, *shir*, as compared with the feminine *shira* used elsewhere (as, for example, in the Benediction preceding the *Hallel*), is significant. According to Rabbinic fantasy, all the songs of this world are feminine in form. That of Messianic times, however, will be more virile: and for this, the masculine term is employed.

THE BLOOD WHICH SHALL BE ACCEPTABLY SPRINKLED: The reference to sprinkling the blood on the walls of the altar is a little alien to modern taste. This ceremony, however, accompanied all sacrifices offered at the Temple of Jerusalem, and the subsequent meal was sanctified by the fact. Granted a carnivorous diet, it is plainly preferable that the slaughter of the animals should take place at the hands of a person fully alive to the responsibilities of his action (the idea which lies at the root of the Jewish *Shechita*), and under conditions which call them to mind. The phrase in the benediction given above is thus, in fact, a prayer for the restoration of the ancient Jewish ideal, when even eating and drinking will once more receive formal sanctification.

WASHING

רחצה

All present wash their hands. The following Benediction is pronounced:

Blessed art Thou, O Lord, our God, King of the Universe, who sanctified us by His commandments and commanded us concerning the washing of the hands.

בָּרוּךְ אַתָּה יְיָ אֱלֹהֵינוּ מֶלֶךְ הָעוֹלָם. אֲשֶׁר קִדְּשָׁנוּ בְּמִצְוֹתָיו וְצִוָּנוּ עַל נְטִילַת יָדָיִם:

The Celebrant distributes a portion of the upper and of the middle cake.

THE BLESSING OVER BREAD

מוציא

Blessed art Thou, O Lord, our God, King of the Universe, the bringer forth of bread out of the earth.

בָּרוּךְ אַתָּה יְיָ אֱלֹהֵינוּ מֶלֶךְ הָעוֹלָם. הַמּוֹצִיא לֶחֶם מִן הָאָרֶץ:

41

THE BLESSING OVER THE MAZZAH

מצה

Blessed art Thou, O Lord, our God, King of the Universe, who sanctified us by His commandments and commanded us concerning the eating of Unleavened Bread.

בָּרוּךְ אַתָּה יְיָ אֱלֹהֵינוּ מֶלֶךְ הָעוֹלָם. אֲשֶׁר קִדְּשָׁנוּ בְּמִצְוֹתָיו וְצִוָּנוּ עַל אֲכִילַת מַצָּה:

BITTER HERB

מרור

The Celebrant distributes Bitter Herb, 'dipped' in Haroseth.

Blessed art Thou, O Lord, our God, King of the Universe, who sanctified us by His commandments and commanded us concerning the eating of Bitter Herb.

בָּרוּךְ אַתָּה יְיָ אֱלֹהֵינוּ מֶלֶךְ הָעוֹלָם. אֲשֶׁר קִדְּשָׁנוּ בְּמִצְוֹתָיו וְצִוָּנוּ עַל אֲכִילַת מָרוֹר:

EATING OF THE UNLEAVENED BREAD: The *Haggadah*, explaining the reason of the Passover Meal, is now ended: and the meal itself now begins with the ceremonial distribution of the *Mazzah*. First, all present rinse their hands, reciting the appropriate Benediction, as is the custom always before breaking bread (the essential hygienics of Jewish practice become manifest time after time during the course of the *Seder*). The Celebrant then distributes a portion of the *Mazzah* to all assembled. Before partaking of it, the usual grace before meals — the Blessing over Bread — is recited. This is immediately followed by the special Blessing upon the eating of Unleavened Bread.

THE BITTER HERB: The Paschal Offering had to be eaten, according to the Scriptural injunction, together with unleavened bread and bitter herb (EX. XII. 8; NUMB. IX. 11) — a symbol of the bitterness of servitude. The next stage of the proceedings is the fulfilment of this ancient usage. For the bitter herb, horseradish is generally used, though every household sometimes has its own tradition. The harshness is, however, mitigated by mingling it with that unique mixture known as *Haroseth* (for which see *Introduction*).

The Celebrant breaks the undermost cake and distributes a portion of it, together with some of the bitter herb, to all of the company. Before partaking of it, the following passage is recited:

In remembrance of the Temple, according to the custom of Hillel.

זֵכֶר לְמִקְדָּשׁ כְּהִלֵּל:

Thus Hillel was accustomed to do when the Temple was still standing: he used to place together some of the Paschal offering, unleavened bread, and bitter herb and eat them as one, to fulfil that which is said: 'Upon unleavened bread and bitter herbs shall they eat it'. (Numb. ix. 11)

כֵּן עָשָׂה הִלֵּל בִּזְמַן שֶׁבֵּית הַמִּקְדָּשׁ הָיָה קַיָּם. הָיָה כּוֹרֵךְ פֶּסַח מַצָּה וּמָרוֹר וְאוֹכֵל בְּיַחַד. לְקַיֵּם מַה שֶׁנֶּאֱמַר: עַל־מַצּוֹת וּמְרוֹרִים יֹאכְלֻהוּ:

PARTAKE OF THE MEAL

שלחן עורך

HILLEL: This saintly scholar of the first century, about whom so many legends and tales have gathered, was accustomed to fulfil literally the Biblical command to eat the Paschal lamb *upon* unleavened bread and bitter herb by placing a portion of each one on top of the other and eating them together, as we read in the *Talmud* (T. B. PES. 115*a*). The next stage sees his example followed: only, since the Paschal lamb is now no longer forthcoming, the bitter herb has to be put between two portions of unleavened bread (taken from the third, undermost cake — the 'Israelite'). It would thus seem that the honour of the comestible invention named after him must be taken from the great Earl of Sandwich, the employer of Samuel Pepys, and vindicated for a Palestinian Rabbi of seventeen centuries before! This constitutes the last formality before the meal: and the *Seder* tray is removed.

43

THE TABLE AS ALTAR

The whole of the *Haggadah* leads up to, and is justified by, the meal, which forms an absolutely integral part of the celebration of the evening. This is natural: for the *Seder* was originally based upon the ceremonies surrounding the consumption of the Paschal lamb, the place of which is now taken by the festal supper. The whole of Rabbinic ideology, indeed, points in this direction. The Table, we are told, now takes the place of the Altar of olden time. The implications are obvious. The proper conduct of man is not to starve himself, but to partake gladly of the good things which God has lavished upon His world: that itself, performed in the right sense, is equivalent to a religious service. But at the same time a spirit of reverence should pervade the board. All immoderation in eating or in drinking is tantamount, almost, to blasphemy. Looseness of language should be avoided. Talk should centre, as far as possible, upon sacred subjects. If three men have eaten together at a table and have spoken there upon matters concerned with the *Torah*, we are informed, it is as though they had eaten at the table of the Almighty. It is by touches such as this that the Rabbis were able to sanctify the commonplaces of existence and to convert every phase of everyday life into an act of Divine service.

THE MEAL

As regards the composition of the *Seder* meal, there is no general tradition. Originally, the main dish was, of course, the Paschal lamb. After the destruction of the Temple, this naturally came to an end; and we are told how the Rabbis of the second century effectively intervened when any attempt was made to imitate the Temple procedure. Local usages, of course, abound. There is an ancient custom to begin the meal with hard-boiled eggs dipped in salt water — a reminiscence of the egg which figures upon the *Seder* tray, and a token in its way of sadness for the destruction of the Temple: for this is the traditional mourning fare. In some families, it is usual to have a meal of one course only, in recollection of the preponderance of the Paschal lamb in the fare when the Temple yet stood. English Jews generally have a fish supper, with one or two special preparations. But all of these usages are strictly local, varying from place to place, and from family to family. The one essential is to have an ample meal, befitting the occasion.

APHIKOMAN

At its conclusion, the half of the Middle *Mazzah*, which had been broken off and secreted at the beginning of the proceedings lest it should be eaten, is distributed amongst the company, each of whom must eat a morsel. It thus serves as what the Greeks used to call ἐπίκωμοι (dessert), this being the most logical explanation of the name by which it is generally known. It represents, in our modern service, the actual Paschal lamb, which was traditionally the last thing to be eaten during the meal, so that its taste and recollection should remain uppermost in the mouth. Accordingly, it is customary to eat nothing further before going to bed: nor should anything be drunk (save for the two statutory cups of wine) excepting water or any similar beverage.

The remaining half of the middle Mazzah, secreted earlier in the evening, is distributed amongst those present, each of whom eats a fragment to conclude the meal.

GRACE   ברך

PSALM CXXVI. When the Lord turned again the captivity of Zion, we were like unto them that dream. Then was our mouth filled with laughter, and our tongue with exultation: then said they among the nations, The Lord hath done great things for them. The Lord hath done great things for us; whereat we rejoiced. Bring back our captivity, O Lord, as the streams in the south. They that sow in tears shall reap in joy. Though he goeth on his way weeping, bearing the store of seed, he shall come back with joy, bearing his sheaves.

תהלים קכ״ו

שִׁיר הַמַּעֲלוֹת ׀ בְּשׁוּב יְיָ אֶת־שִׁיבַת
צִיּוֹן הָיִינוּ כְּחֹלְמִים: אָז יִמָּלֵא שְׂחוֹק פִּינוּ
וּלְשׁוֹנֵנוּ רִנָּה אָז יֹאמְרוּ בַגּוֹיִם הִגְדִּיל יְיָ
לַעֲשׂוֹת עִם־אֵלֶּה: הִגְדִּיל יְיָ לַעֲשׂוֹת עִמָּנוּ
הָיִינוּ שְׂמֵחִים: שׁוּבָה יְיָ אֶת־שְׁבִיתֵנוּ
כַּאֲפִיקִים בַּנֶּגֶב: הַזֹּרְעִים בְּדִמְעָה בְּרִנָּה
יִקְצֹרוּ: הָלוֹךְ יֵלֵךְ וּבָכֹה נֹשֵׂא מֶשֶׁךְ־
הַזָּרַע בֹּא־יָבֹא בְרִנָּה נֹשֵׂא אֲלֻמֹּתָיו:

THE GRACE which follows is the ordinary 'Blessing over the Repast' recited at the close of all meals: excepting that the cup of wine, which is generally optional, is at this service obligatory. The formula as we have it goes back traditionally to the time of Abraham, the latest additions belonging, according to the same account, to the period following the Palestinian revolt of 132—5. Certainly, it is of very considerable antiquity, and the tale which fixes its completion in the second century is not wide of the mark. The invocations to 'the All Merciful' towards the end are susceptible of a vast amount of local variation, especially as regards that calling down blessings on the Master of the House: and it is an æsthetic joy to hear the delicate hyperbole in which an Oriental Jew expresses at this stage his gratitude to his host.

*If three males or more are present, the following introductory phrases are added. When
ten or more are present, the words in brackets are interpolated.
He who is to say Grace begins:*

My Masters, let us say the Blessing.

רַבּוֹתַי נְבָרֵךְ:

May the Name of the Lord be blessed
from this time forth and for ever.

יְהִי שֵׁם יְיָ מְבֹרָךְ מֵעַתָּה וְעַד־עוֹלָם:

Let us bless Him (our God) of whose
bounty we have partaken.

בִּרְשׁוּת רַבּוֹתַי נְבָרֵךְ [אֱלֹהֵינוּ] שֶׁאָכַלְנוּ
מִשֶּׁלּוֹ:

Blessed be He (our God) of whose
bounty we have partaken and through
whose goodness we live.

בָּרוּךְ [אֱלֹהֵינוּ] שֶׁאָכַלְנוּ מִשֶּׁלּוֹ וּבְטוּבוֹ
חָיִינוּ:

Blessed art Thou, O Lord,
our God, King of the Uni-
verse: who sustaineth the
whole world in His goodness,
in grace, lovingkindness, and
mercy. 'He giveth bread to
all flesh: for His mercy endureth for ever' (Ps. cxxxvi. 25).
And through His goodness,
which is ever great, suste-

בָּרוּךְ אַתָּה יְיָ אֱלֹהֵינוּ מֶלֶךְ
הָעוֹלָם הַזָּן אֶת־הָעוֹלָם כֻּלּוֹ
בְּטוּבוֹ בְּחֵן בְּחֶסֶד וּבְרַחֲמִים
הוּא נוֹתֵן לֶחֶם לְכָל־בָּשָׂר כִּי
לְעוֹלָם חַסְדּוֹ: וּבְטוּבוֹ הַגָּדוֹל
תָּמִיד לֹא־חָסַר לָנוּ וְאַל יֶחְסַר

46

nance hath never failed us, nor will fail us, for ever and ever, for His great Name's sake. For he sustaineth and supporteth all, and doth good to all, and prepareth sustenance to all His creatures which He hath created. Blessed art Thou, O Lord, who sustainest all.

לָנוּ מָזוֹן לְעוֹלָם וָעֶד ⸱ בַּעֲבוּר שְׁמוֹ הַגָּדוֹל ⸱ כִּי הוּא זָן וּמְפַרְנֵס לַכֹּל וּמֵטִיב לַכֹּל וּמֵכִין מָזוֹן לְכָל בְּרִיּוֹתָיו אֲשֶׁר בָּרָא ⸱ בָּרוּךְ אַתָּה יְיָ הַזָּן אֶת־הַכֹּל׃

Let us render thanks unto Thee, O Lord, our God, because Thou didst give as an inheritance to our fathers a land which is pleasant, goodly, and ample: and because Thou didst bring us forth, O Lord, our God, from the land of Egypt, and didst redeem us from the house of bondage: and for Thy covenant which Thou didst seal in our flesh, and for Thy law which Thou hast taught us, and for Thy statutes which Thou hast made known unto us, and for the life, grace, and lovingkindness wherewith Thou hast favoured us, and for the partaking of this sustenance wherewith Thou dost sustain and support us continually — on every day, and at every time, and in every hour.

נוֹדֶה לְךָ יְיָ אֱלֹהֵינוּ עַל שֶׁהִנְחַלְתָּ לַאֲבוֹתֵינוּ אֶרֶץ חֶמְדָּה טוֹבָה וּרְחָבָה ⸱ וְעַל שֶׁהוֹצֵאתָנוּ יְיָ אֱלֹהֵינוּ מֵאֶרֶץ מִצְרַיִם וּפְדִיתָנוּ מִבֵּית עֲבָדִים ⸱ וְעַל בְּרִיתְךָ שֶׁחָתַמְתָּ בִּבְשָׂרֵנוּ וְעַל תּוֹרָתְךָ שֶׁלִּמַּדְתָּנוּ וְעַל חֻקֶּיךָ שֶׁהוֹדַעְתָּנוּ ⸱ וְעַל חַיִּים חֵן וָחֶסֶד שֶׁחוֹנַנְתָּנוּ ⸱ וְעַל אֲכִילַת מָזוֹן שָׁאַתָּה זָן וּמְפַרְנֵס אוֹתָנוּ תָּמִיד בְּכָל־יוֹם וּבְכָל־עֵת וּבְכָל־שָׁעָה׃

For all this, O Lord, our God, we render thanks to Thee and bless Thee. Blessed be Thy Name in the mouth of all that lives, continually and for evermore: as it is written, 'And thou shalt eat, and be satisfied, and shalt bless the Lord thy God for the good land which He hath given thee' (DEUT. VIII. 10). Blessed art Thou, O Lord, for the Land and for the sustenance.

וְעַל הַכֹּל יְיָ אֱלֹהֵינוּ אֲנַחְנוּ מוֹדִים לָךְ וּמְבָרְכִים אוֹתָךְ יִתְבָּרַךְ שִׁמְךָ בְּפִי כָל־חַי תָּמִיד לְעוֹלָם וָעֶד׃ כַּכָּתוּב וְאָכַלְתָּ וְשָׂבָעְתָּ וּבֵרַכְתָּ אֶת־יְיָ אֱלֹהֶיךָ עַל־הָאָרֶץ הַטֹּבָה אֲשֶׁר נָתַן לָךְ ⸱ בָּרוּךְ אַתָּה יְיָ עַל־הָאָרֶץ וְעַל־הַמָּזוֹן׃

47

Have mercy, O Lord, our God, upon Israel Thy people, and upon Jerusalem Thy city, and upon Zion the abiding-place of Thy glory, and upon the kingdom of the house of David, Thine anointed, and upon the great and holy House which is called by Thy Name. O our God, our Father! do Thou pasture us, sustain us, support us, maintain us, and deliver us! Deliver us, O Lord, our God, speedily from all our troubles. And we beseech Thee, O Lord, our God, make us not dependent upon the gifts of flesh and blood, nor upon their loans, but only upon Thy full, open, holy, and ample hand: so that we may not be ashamed nor abashed for ever and ever.

רַחֵם יְיָ אֱלֹהֵינוּ עַל־יִשְׂרָאֵל
עַמֶּךָ וְעַל־יְרוּשָׁלַיִם עִירֶךָ
וְעַל־צִיּוֹן מִשְׁכַּן כְּבוֹדֶךָ וְעַל־
מַלְכוּת בֵּית דָּוִד מְשִׁיחֶךָ וְעַל־
הַבַּיִת הַגָּדוֹל וְהַקָּדוֹשׁ שֶׁנִּקְרָא
שִׁמְךָ עָלָיו: אֱלֹהֵינוּ אָבִינוּ
רְעֵנוּ זוּנֵנוּ פַּרְנְסֵנוּ וְכַלְכְּלֵנוּ
וְהַרְוִיחֵנוּ וְהַרְוַח־לָנוּ יְיָ אֱלֹהֵינוּ
מְהֵרָה מִכָּל־צָרוֹתֵינוּ: וְנָא אַל־
תַּצְרִיכֵנוּ יְיָ אֱלֹהֵינוּ לֹא לִידֵי
מַתְּנַת בָּשָׂר וָדָם וְלֹא לִידֵי
הַלְוָאָתָם. כִּי־אִם לְיָדְךָ הַמְּלֵאָה
הַפְּתוּחָה וְהַקְּדוֹשָׁה וְהָרְחָבָה
שֶׁלֹּא נֵבוֹשׁ וְלֹא נִכָּלֵם לְעוֹלָם
וָעֶד:

The following paragraph is added upon the Sabbath:

Be pleased, O Lord, our God, to prosper us by Thy precepts, and especially by the precept concerning the seventh day, this great and holy Sabbath. For this day is great and holy before Thee, that we may rest thereon and repose thereon in love, according to Thy gracious precept. By Thy grace, O Lord, our God, grant us repose, that there may be no trouble nor sorrow nor lamentation upon our day of rest: and cause us to see the con-

רְצֵה וְהַחֲלִיצֵנוּ יְיָ אֱלֹהֵינוּ בְּמִצְוֹתֶיךָ
וּבְמִצְוַת יוֹם הַשְּׁבִיעִי הַשַּׁבָּת הַגָּדוֹל
וְהַקָּדוֹשׁ הַזֶּה כִּי יוֹם זֶה גָּדוֹל וְקָדוֹשׁ הוּא
לְפָנֶיךָ לִשְׁבָּת־בּוֹ וְלָנוּחַ בּוֹ בְּאַהֲבָה
כְּמִצְוַת רְצוֹנֶךָ: בִּרְצוֹנְךָ הָנִיחַ לָנוּ יְיָ
אֱלֹהֵינוּ שֶׁלֹּא תְהִי צָרָה וְיָגוֹן וַאֲנָחָה
בְּיוֹם מְנוּחָתֵנוּ וְהַרְאֵנוּ יְיָ אֱלֹהֵינוּ בְּנֶחָמַת

e

solation of Zion Thy city, and the building of Jerusalem Thy holy city: for Thou art He who is Lord of redemption and Lord of consolation.

צִיּוֹן עִירֶךָ וּבְבִנְיַן יְרוּשָׁלַיִם עִיר קָדְשֶׁךָ, כִּי אַתָּה הוּא בַּעַל הַיְשׁוּעוֹת וּבַעַל הַנֶּחָמוֹת:

Our God, and God of our Fathers! May there ascend, and come, and arrive, and be seen, and accepted, and heard, and visited, and remembered — our remembrance, and our visitation, and the remembrance of our Fathers, and the remembrance of the anointed Messiah, son of David Thy servant, and the remembrance of Jerusalem Thy holy city, and the remembrance of the whole of Thy people the house of Israel: for deliverance, and for good, and for grace, and for lovingkindness, and for mercy, and for life, and for peace, before Thee, upon this day, the Feast of Unleavened Bread. Remember us thereon, O Lord, our God, for good, and visit us thereon for a blessing, and save us thereon for life: through tidings of redemption and mercy pity us and show us grace, and be merciful unto us and redeem us, for to Thee are our eyes turned, for Thou art a gracious and merciful God and King.

אֱלֹהֵינוּ וֵאלֹהֵי אֲבוֹתֵינוּ. יַעֲלֶה וְיָבֹא וְיַגִּיעַ וְיֵרָאֶה וְיֵרָצֶה וְיִשָּׁמַע וְיִפָּקֵד וְיִזָּכֵר זִכְרוֹנֵנוּ וּפִקְדוֹנֵנוּ. וְזִכְרוֹן אֲבוֹתֵינוּ וְזִכְרוֹן מָשִׁיחַ בֶּן דָּוִד עַבְדֶּךָ. וְזִכְרוֹן יְרוּשָׁלַיִם עִיר קָדְשֶׁךָ. וְזִכְרוֹן כָּל־עַמְּךָ בֵּית יִשְׂרָאֵל לְפָנֶיךָ. לִפְלֵטָה, לְטוֹבָה, לְחֵן וּלְחֶסֶד וּלְרַחֲמִים לְחַיִּים וּלְשָׁלוֹם בְּיוֹם חַג הַמַּצּוֹת הַזֶּה. זָכְרֵנוּ יְיָ אֱלֹהֵינוּ בּוֹ לְטוֹבָה. וּפָקְדֵנוּ בוֹ לִבְרָכָה. וְהוֹשִׁיעֵנוּ בוֹ לְחַיִּים. וּבִדְבַר יְשׁוּעָה וְרַחֲמִים חוּס וְחָנֵּנוּ. וְרַחֵם עָלֵינוּ וְהוֹשִׁיעֵנוּ. כִּי אֵלֶיךָ עֵינֵינוּ. כִּי אֵל מֶלֶךְ חַנּוּן וְרַחוּם אָתָּה:

49

And build Thou Jerusalem
the holy city speedily in our
days: blessed art Thou, O
Lord, Rebuilder, in His mercy, of Jerusalem: Amen!

Blessed art Thou, O Lord, our God, King
of the Universe: O God, our Father, our
King, our Mighty One, our Creator, our
Redeemer, our Maker, our Holy One,
the Holy One of Jacob: our Shepherd,
the Shepherd of Israel: the good King,
who doth good to all, who, upon every
day did good, doth good, and will do
good unto us. He hath bestowed, He
doth bestow, He will bestow benefits
upon us always, for grace, lovingkindness, mercy and deliverance: protection,
prosperity, blessing, salvation, comfort,
support, sustenance, mercy, life, peace
and all good; and all good may He never
let us lack!

May the All-Merciful reign over us, for
ever and ever!

May the All-Merciful be blessed in
heaven and on earth!

May the All-Merciful be praised for all
generations, and may He be glorified
through us for all ages, and exalted
through us for ever, and for all eternity!

May the All-Merciful grant us honour-
able sustenance!

May the All-Merciful break the yoke
from off our neck, and may He lead us
upright to our land!

May the All-Merciful send an ample
blessing to this house, and upon this
table whereon we have eaten!

וּבְנֵה יְרוּשָׁלַיִם עִיר הַקֹּדֶשׁ
בִּמְהֵרָה בְיָמֵינוּ: בָּרוּךְ אַתָּה יְיָ,
בּוֹנֵה בְרַחֲמָיו יְרוּשָׁלָיִם. אָמֵן:

בָּרוּךְ אַתָּה יְיָ, אֱלֹהֵינוּ מֶלֶךְ הָעוֹלָם.
הָאֵל אָבִינוּ מַלְכֵּנוּ אַדִּירֵנוּ בּוֹרְאֵנוּ גֹּאֲלֵנוּ
יוֹצְרֵנוּ קְדוֹשֵׁנוּ קְדוֹשׁ יַעֲקֹב רוֹעֵנוּ רוֹעֵה
יִשְׂרָאֵל הַמֶּלֶךְ הַטּוֹב וְהַמֵּטִיב לַכֹּל שֶׁבְּכָל
יוֹם וָיוֹם הוּא הֵטִיב הוּא מֵטִיב הוּא
יֵטִיב לָנוּ: הוּא גְמָלָנוּ הוּא גוֹמְלֵנוּ הוּא
יִגְמְלֵנוּ לָעַד לְחֵן לְחֶסֶד וּלְרַחֲמִים וּלְרֶוַח
הַצָּלָה וְהַצְלָחָה בְּרָכָה וִישׁוּעָה נֶחָמָה
פַּרְנָסָה וְכַלְכָּלָה וְרַחֲמִים וְחַיִּים וְשָׁלוֹם
וְכָל־טוֹב וּמִכָּל־טוּב לְעוֹלָם אַל יְחַסְּרֵנוּ:

הָרַחֲמָן הוּא יִמְלוֹךְ עָלֵינוּ לְעוֹלָם וָעֶד:

הָרַחֲמָן הוּא יִתְבָּרַךְ בַּשָּׁמַיִם וּבָאָרֶץ:

הָרַחֲמָן הוּא יִשְׁתַּבַּח לְדוֹר דּוֹרִים
וְיִתְפָּאַר־בָּנוּ לָנֶצַח נְצָחִים וְיִתְהַדַּר־בָּנוּ
לָעַד וּלְעוֹלְמֵי עוֹלָמִים:

הָרַחֲמָן הוּא יְפַרְנְסֵנוּ בְּכָבוֹד:

הָרַחֲמָן הוּא יִשְׁבּוֹר עֻלֵּנוּ מֵעַל צַוָּארֵנוּ
וְהוּא יוֹלִיכֵנוּ קוֹמְמִיּוּת לְאַרְצֵנוּ:

הָרַחֲמָן הוּא יִשְׁלַח בְּרָכָה מְרֻבָּה בַּבַּיִת
הַזֶּה וְעַל שֻׁלְחָן זֶה שֶׁאָכַלְנוּ עָלָיו:

50

May the All-Merciful send us Elijah the Prophet (may he be remembered for good!), who shall proclaim us good tidings, salvation and comfort.

הָרַחֲמָן הוּא יִשְׁלַח־לָנוּ אֶת־אֵלִיָּהוּ הַנָּבִיא זָכוּר לַטּוֹב וִיבַשֶּׂר־לָנוּ בְּשׂוֹרוֹת טוֹבוֹת יְשׁוּעוֹת וְנֶחָמוֹת:

The following may be modified according to circumstances:

May the All-Merciful bless all that sit here — them, their households, their offspring, and all that is theirs: us, and all that is ours. As our fathers Abraham, Isaac, and Jacob were blessed 'in all' (GEN. XXIV. 1), 'of all' (XXVII. 33), 'in respect of all' (XXXIII. 11) so may He bless us all together with a perfect blessing: and let us say, Amen!

הָרַחֲמָן הוּא יְבָרֵךְ אֶת־כָּל־הַיּוֹשְׁבִים פֹּה אוֹתָם וְאֶת־בֵּיתָם וְאֶת־זַרְעָם וְאֶת־כָּל־אֲשֶׁר לָהֶם אוֹתָנוּ וְאֶת־כָּל־אֲשֶׁר לָנוּ כְּמוֹ שֶׁנִּתְבָּרְכוּ אֲבוֹתֵינוּ אַבְרָהָם יִצְחָק וְיַעֲקֹב בַּכֹּל מִכֹּל כֹּל. כֵּן יְבָרֵךְ אוֹתָנוּ כֻּלָּנוּ יַחַד בִּבְרָכָה שְׁלֵמָה וְנֹאמַר אָמֵן:

Upon high, may there be pleaded merit for us, which shall be for a store of peace: and may we receive a blessing from the Lord, and righteousness from the God of our salvation, so that we may find grace and good understanding in the sight of God and man!

בַּמָּרוֹם יְלַמְּדוּ עָלֵינוּ זְכוּת שֶׁתְּהִי לְמִשְׁמֶרֶת שָׁלוֹם · וְנִשָּׂא בְרָכָה מֵאֵת יְיָ וּצְדָקָה מֵאֱלֹהֵי יִשְׁעֵנוּ: וְנִמְצָא־חֵן וְשֵׂכֶל טוֹב בְּעֵינֵי אֱלֹהִים וְאָדָם:

On the Sabbath, the following paragraph is added:

May the All-Merciful cause us to inherit that day which shall be altogether Sabbath and repose, in life everlasting!

הָרַחֲמָן הוּא יַנְחִילֵנוּ יוֹם שֶׁכֻּלּוֹ שַׁבָּת וּמְנוּחָה לְחַיֵּי הָעוֹלָמִים:

May the All-Merciful cause us to inherit that day which shall be altogether Holy-Day!

הָרַחֲמָן הוּא יַנְחִילֵנוּ יוֹם שֶׁכֻּלּוֹ טוֹב:

May the All-Merciful make us worthy of the days of the Messiah and the life of the world to come!

הָרַחֲמָן הוּא זַכֵּנוּ לִימוֹת הַמָּשִׁיחַ וּלְחַיֵּי הָעוֹלָם הַבָּא:

51

'He is a tower of deliverance to His king, and sheweth lovingkindness to His anointed, to David and to his seed, for evermore!' (II Sam. xxii. 51) He who maketh peace in His high places, may He make peace for us and for all Israel: and say ye, Amen!

מִגְדּוֹל יְשׁוּעוֹת מַלְכּוֹ וְעֹשֶׂה חֶסֶד לִמְשִׁיחוֹ לְדָוִד וּלְזַרְעוֹ עַד־עוֹלָם. עֹשֶׂה שָׁלוֹם בִּמְרוֹמָיו הוּא יַעֲשֶׂה שָׁלוֹם עָלֵינוּ וְעַל־כָּל־יִשְׂרָאֵל וְאִמְרוּ אָמֵן:

'Fear the Lord, ye His saints, for there is no want to them that fear Him. The young lions do lack, and suffer hunger, but they that seek the Lord shall not want any good thing' (Ps. xxxiv. 9—10). 'O give thanks unto the Lord, for He is good, for His mercy endureth for ever' (Ps. cxviii. 1). 'Thou openest Thy hand and satisfiest every living thing with favour' (Ps. cxlv. 16). 'Blessed is the man that trusteth in the Lord, and whose trust the Lord is' (Ps. xl. 4). 'I have been young and now am old; yet have I not seen the righteous forsaken nor his seed begging their bread' (Ps. xxxvii. 25). 'The Lord will give strength unto His people: the Lord will bless His people with peace' (Ps. xxix. 11).

יְראוּ אֶת־יְיָ קְדוֹשָׁיו כִּי אֵין מַחְסוֹר לִירֵאָיו: כְּפִירִים רָשׁוּ וְרָעֵבוּ וְדֹרְשֵׁי יְיָ לֹא־ יַחְסְרוּ כָל־טוֹב: הוֹדוּ לַיְיָ כִּי־טוֹב כִּי לְעוֹלָם חַסְדּוֹ: פּוֹתֵחַ אֶת־יָדֶךָ וּמַשְׂבִּיעַ לְכָל־חַי רָצוֹן: בָּרוּךְ הַגֶּבֶר אֲשֶׁר יִבְטַח בַּיְיָ וְהָיָה יְיָ מִבְטַחוֹ: נַעַר הָיִיתִי גַּם־ זָקַנְתִּי וְלֹא־רָאִיתִי צַדִּיק נֶעֱזָב וְזַרְעוֹ מְבַקֶּשׁ־לָחֶם: יְיָ עֹז לְעַמּוֹ יִתֵּן יְיָ יְבָרֵךְ אֶת־עַמּוֹ בַשָּׁלוֹם:

Blessed art Thou, O Lord, our God, King of the Universe, Creator of the fruit of the vine.

בָּרוּךְ אַתָּה יְיָ אֱלֹהֵינוּ מֶלֶךְ הָעוֹלָם. בּוֹרֵא פְּרִי הַגָּפֶן:

The third cup of wine is here drunk.

The door is opened, and the fourth and last cup of wine (the Cup of Redemption) is filled: an additional cup, known as the Cup of Elijah, is placed on the table at this stage. Meanwhile, the following verses are recited:

'Pour out Thy wrath upon the heathen that have not known Thee, and upon the kingdoms that have not called upon Thy Name: for they have devoured Jacob and laid waste his dwelling place' (Ps. lxxix. 6). 'Pour out upon them Thy indignation and let Thy fierce anger overtake them' (Ps. lxix, 25). 'Pursue them in wrath and destroy them from under the heavens of the Lord' (Lam. iii. 66).

שְׁפֹךְ חֲמָתְךָ אֶל־הַגּוֹיִם אֲשֶׁר לֹא־יְדָעוּךָ וְעַל־מַמְלָכוֹת אֲשֶׁר בְּשִׁמְךָ לֹא קָרָאוּ: כִּי אָכַל אֶת־יַעֲקֹב וְאֶת־נָוֵהוּ הֵשַׁמּוּ: שְׁפָךְ־עֲלֵיהֶם זַעְמֶךָ וַחֲרוֹן אַפְּךָ יַשִּׂיגֵם: תִּרְדֹּף בְּאַף וְתַשְׁמִידֵם מִתַּחַת שְׁמֵי יְיָ:

No part of the Passover Service has aroused so much criticism as the above passage: 'Pour out thy wrath upon the nations....' It is, one is variously informed, vengeful, vindictive, and unworthy of a people that calls itself civilized. Its detractors generally overlook the fact, however, that it is not a prayer, but a quotation — or, rather, a series of quotations (Ps. lxxix, 6; lxix, 25; Lam. iii, 66). Moreover, if it were intended as an imprecation upon the Jews' neighbours, it is incomprehensible why it is precisely at this passage that the door is opened, giving every opportunity for eavesdropping and revenge. As a matter of fact, the significance of the passage is something quite different, though it has become obscured in the course of the ages.

The third cup of wine has been drained. The *Hallel*, or Thanksgiving Psalms (traditionally recited over wine), are to be continued. The goblets have therefore to be filled again, for the fourth and last time, there being now added to them one associated with the name of Elijah. As the wine is being poured out, it is by no means unnatural to repeat the symbolic verse: '*Pour out* Thy wrath upon the heathen that hath not known Thee, and upon the kingdoms that have not called upon Thy Name.' It is an obvious enough verse to choose to accompany the action (one could cite a score of similar instances in Jewish practice), and one which, moreover, serves as an apt introduction to the second part of the *Hallel*, which otherwise starts with unusual abruptness. In many old manuscripts this initial verse alone figures: and the whole passage is still printed, in those editions which follow close upon traditional lines, without any differentiation in space or in type from what follows after, proving their essential unity.

53

Ps. cxv. Not unto us, O Lord, but unto Thy Name give glory, for Thy lovingkindness and for Thy truth's sake. Wherefore should the nations say, Where, then, is their God? But our God is in the heavens, He doeth whatsoever He pleaseth. Their idols are silver and gold, the work of men's hands. They have mouths, but they speak not; eyes have they, but they see not. They have ears, but they hear not; noses have they, but they smell not. As for their hands, they touch not, as for their feet, they walk not; they give no sound through their throat. They that make them shall be like unto them; yea, everyone that trusteth in them. O Israel, trust thou in the Lord: He is their help and their shield. O house of Aaron, trust in the Lord: He is their help and their shield. Ye that fear the Lord, trust in the Lord: He is their help and their shield.

לֹא לָנוּ יְיָ לֹא לָנוּ כִּי לְשִׁמְךָ תֵּן כָּבוֹד
עַל־חַסְדְּךָ עַל־אֲמִתֶּךָ: לָמָה יֹאמְרוּ הַגּוֹיִם
אַיֵּה־נָא אֱלֹהֵיהֶם: וֵאלֹהֵינוּ בַשָּׁמַיִם כֹּל
אֲשֶׁר־חָפֵץ עָשָׂה: עֲצַבֵּיהֶם כֶּסֶף וְזָהָב
מַעֲשֵׂה יְדֵי אָדָם: פֶּה־לָהֶם וְלֹא יְדַבֵּרוּ
עֵינַיִם לָהֶם וְלֹא יִרְאוּ: אָזְנַיִם לָהֶם וְלֹא
יִשְׁמָעוּ אַף לָהֶם וְלֹא יְרִיחוּן: יְדֵיהֶם וְלֹא
יְמִישׁוּן רַגְלֵיהֶם וְלֹא יְהַלֵּכוּ לֹא יֶהְגּוּ
בִּגְרוֹנָם: כְּמוֹהֶם יִהְיוּ עֹשֵׂיהֶם כֹּל אֲשֶׁר־
בֹּטֵחַ בָּהֶם: יִשְׂרָאֵל בְּטַח בַּיְיָ עֶזְרָם
וּמָגִנָּם הוּא: בֵּית אַהֲרֹן בִּטְחוּ בַיְיָ עֶזְרָם
וּמָגִנָּם הוּא: יִרְאֵי יְיָ בִּטְחוּ בַיְיָ עֶזְרָם
וּמָגִנָּם הוּא:

But the Jew was only human: and it is not altogether remarkable if, during the period of mediæval persecution, some persons felt inclined to complete the passage from which the quotation came, or even to add a few other verses of similar import. It is a curious study in religious psychology to see how the formula becomes more and more imprecatory in those countries where the lot of the Jew was most miserable. But even so (and it is most important to note this point), the reference is specifically to idolators, who know not God and do not call upon His Name. Our 'Ashkenazic' formula occupies a middle place between the milder Spanish and the more élaborately maledictory Byzantine and Provençal rites.

Ultimately, the symbolic application of the verse came to be forgotten. The pouring out of the wine was transferred until after the completion of this passage, thus entirely altering its significance: while the mystical opening of the door gave the passage an exaggerated prominence. This was accentuated in the old *Haggadoth* by the typographical or illuminatory splendour with which it was adorned, in order to mark the beginning of the second half of the service. By the simple process, supported in many manuscripts and a few printed editions, of re-transferring the pouring out of the wine to its original position, the true significance of the passage is restored. The custom of opening the door when the feast is ended has given rise to a good deal of misplaced learning and superfluous sentimentality. We are told by the romantic school that this became usual in the worst period of mediæval persecution, when the blood-accusation was rife, in order to manifest conclusively to the outside world that the body of a Christian child was not concealed about the house. But assuredly the opening of the door would have given the Gentile mob the ideal opportunity (if it so desired) of introducing evidence of the crime. Moreover, such procedure might well have been taken as proof of guilt rather than of innocence (not that, as a matter of fact, proof, or even evidence, was necessary in the Middle Ages on any occasion when Jew-baiting was desired): for it is obvious that the proper time to demonstrate that Christian blood was not necessary for the Passover celebration was before the meal rather than after it.

54

The Lord hath been mindful of us: He will bless, He will bless the house of Israel; He will bless the house of Aaron. He will bless them that fear the Lord, both small and great. May the Lord increase you, you and your children. Blessed are ye of the Lord, who made heaven and earth. The heavens are the heavens of the Lord; but the earth hath He given to the children of men. The dead praise not the Lord, neither any that go down in silence; but we will bless the Lord from this time forth and for evermore. Praise ye the Lord.

יְיָ זְכָרָנוּ יְבָרֵךְ יְבָרֵךְ אֶת־בֵּית
יִשְׂרָאֵל יְבָרֵךְ אֶת־בֵּית אַהֲרֹן:
יְבָרֵךְ יִרְאֵי יְיָ הַקְּטַנִּים עִם
הַגְּדֹלִים: יֹסֵף יְיָ עֲלֵיכֶם עֲלֵיכֶם
וְעַל־בְּנֵיכֶם: בְּרוּכִים אַתֶּם לַיְיָ
עֹשֵׂה שָׁמַיִם וָאָרֶץ: הַשָּׁמַיִם
שָׁמַיִם לַיְיָ וְהָאָרֶץ נָתַן לִבְנֵי
אָדָם: לֹא הַמֵּתִים יְהַלְלוּ־יָהּ
וְלֹא כָּל־יֹרְדֵי דוּמָה: וַאֲנַחְנוּ
נְבָרֵךְ יָהּ מֵעַתָּה וְעַד־עוֹלָם
הַלְלוּיָהּ:

Classical scholars point to the Roman parallel of laying a place at table and setting aside a portion of food for the benefit of the household god. The similarity is indeed striking. However, this can hardly be imagined to be the origin of the custom at present under consideration, if only because of the strangely illogical point at which the formality is executed, at the close of the meal, and not at the beginning.

The true explanation is simple enough. Perhaps, in origin, the door was opened in hopes of finding some belated visitor, and the cup of wine was poured out on his behalf. But, in the course of time, this ceremony came to receive a mystical significance. The first part of the *Haggadah* has dealt more or less historically with the Exodus — the Passover of Egypt. The second half concentrates to an increasing extent upon the Passover of the Future — the redemption that is to be. For on Passover Night (according to an old and beautiful legend) Elijah the Tishbite is to come to herald the Messiah — Elijah, the undying prophet, who was snatched up to heaven in a fiery chariot, and who is eternally abroad among the people for whom he so laboured of old, revealing the secrets of Israel's future to many a mystic, and present in the chair set apart for his use on every occasion on which a child is initiated into the covenant of Judaism. What more natural at this stage than that the door should be opened to receive him, while a goblet of wine is poured out in his honour? And, moreover, the opening of the door was itself an indication of the Divine protection: for, according to the Rabbis, this was indeed a 'Night of Watching unto the Lord' (Ex. XII. 42), when Israel 'throughout all their generations' were to be secure against all molestation. It is true that this confidence was occasionally belied; but the fact never made the Jew waver in his allegiance. The foregoing interpretation of this symbolism is confirmed by the mediæval artistic convention in which this passage of the *Haggadah* is generally adorned by a representation of Elijah the prophet announcing the promised Deliverer in front of an open door — the door which Israel leaves open at this stage on his behalf.

55

Ps. cxvi. I love the Lord, because He heareth my voice and my supplications. Because He hath inclined His ear unto me, therefore will I call upon Him as long as I live. The cords of death had encompassed me, and the straits of the grave had come upon me: I found trouble and sorrow. Then I called upon the Name of the Lord: O Lord, I beseech Thee, deliver my soul. Gracious is the Lord and righteous: yea, our God is merciful. The Lord guardeth the simple: I was brought low, and He saved me. Return unto thy rest, O my soul; for the Lord hath dealt bountifully with thee. For Thou hast delivered my soul from death, mine eyes from tears, my feet from falling. I shall walk before the Lord in the land of the living. I kept my faith in God even when I spake, I am greatly afflicted; even when I said in my haste, All men are liars.

What can I render unto the Lord for all His benefits towards me? I will lift the cup of salvation, and call upon the Name of the Lord. I will pay my vows unto the Lord, yea, in the presence of all His people. Precious in the sight of the Lord is the death of His loving ones. Ah, Lord, truly I am Thy servant: I am Thy servant, the son of Thy handmaid; Thou hast loosed my bonds. I will offer to Thee the sacrifice of thanksgiving, and will call upon the Name of the Lord. I will pay my vows unto the Lord, yea, in the presence of all His people; in the courts of the

אָהַבְתִּי כִּי־יִשְׁמַע יְיָ אֶת־קוֹלִי תַּחֲנוּנָי:
כִּי־הִטָּה אָזְנוֹ לִי וּבְיָמַי אֶקְרָא: אֲפָפוּנִי
חֶבְלֵי־מָוֶת וּמְצָרֵי שְׁאוֹל מְצָאוּנִי צָרָה
וְיָגוֹן אֶמְצָא: וּבְשֵׁם יְיָ אֶקְרָא אָנָּה יְיָ
מַלְּטָה נַפְשִׁי: חַנּוּן יְיָ וְצַדִּיק וֵאלֹהֵינוּ
מְרַחֵם: שֹׁמֵר פְּתָאיִם יְיָ דַּלֹּתִי וְלִי יְהוֹשִׁיעַ:
שׁוּבִי נַפְשִׁי לִמְנוּחָיְכִי כִּי־יְיָ גָּמַל עָלָיְכִי:
כִּי חִלַּצְתָּ נַפְשִׁי מִמָּוֶת אֶת־עֵינִי מִן־
דִּמְעָה אֶת־רַגְלִי מִדֶּחִי: אֶתְהַלֵּךְ לִפְנֵי יְיָ
בְּאַרְצוֹת הַחַיִּים: הֶאֱמַנְתִּי כִּי אֲדַבֵּר אֲנִי
עָנִיתִי מְאֹד: אֲנִי אָמַרְתִּי בְחָפְזִי כָּל־
הָאָדָם כֹּזֵב:

מָה־אָשִׁיב לַיְיָ כָּל־תַּגְמוּלוֹהִי
עָלָי: כּוֹס־יְשׁוּעוֹת אֶשָּׂא וּבְשֵׁם
יְיָ אֶקְרָא: נְדָרַי לַיְיָ אֲשַׁלֵּם
נֶגְדָה־נָּא לְכָל־עַמּוֹ: יָקָר
בְּעֵינֵי יְיָ הַמָּוְתָה לַחֲסִידָיו:
אָנָּה יְיָ כִּי אֲנִי עַבְדֶּךָ אֲנִי
עַבְדְּךָ בֶּן־אֲמָתֶךָ פִּתַּחְתָּ
לְמוֹסֵרָי: לְךָ אֶזְבַּח זֶבַח תּוֹדָה
וּבְשֵׁם יְיָ אֶקְרָא: נְדָרַי לַיְיָ
אֲשַׁלֵּם נֶגְדָה־נָּא לְכָל־עַמּוֹ:

Lord's house, in the midst of thee, O Jerusalem. Praise ye the Lord.

בְּחַצְרוֹת בֵּית יְיָ בְּתוֹכֵכִי יְרוּשָׁלָ͏ִם הַלְלוּיָהּ:

Ps. cxvii. O praise the Lord, all ye nations; laud him, all ye peoples; for his lovingkindness is mighty over us, and the truth of the Lord endureth for ever. Praise ye the Lord.

הַלְלוּ אֶת־יְיָ כָּל־גּוֹיִם שַׁבְּחוּהוּ כָּל־הָאֻמִּים: כִּי גָבַר עָלֵינוּ חַסְדּוֹ וֶאֱמֶת־יְיָ לְעוֹלָם הַלְלוּיָהּ:

Ps. cxviii. O give thanks unto the Lord; for he is good:
    for his lovingkindness endureth for ever.

הוֹדוּ לַיְיָ כִּי־טוֹב כִּי לְעוֹלָם חַסְדּוֹ:

O let Israel say,
    that his lovingkindness endureth for ever.

יֹאמַר־נָא יִשְׂרָאֵל כִּי לְעוֹלָם חַסְדּוֹ:

O let the house of Aaron say,
    that his lovingkindness endureth for ever.

יֹאמְרוּ־נָא בֵית־אַהֲרֹן כִּי לְעוֹלָם חַסְדּוֹ:

O let them that fear the Lord say,
    that his lovingkindness endureth for ever.

יֹאמְרוּ־נָא יִרְאֵי יְיָ כִּי לְעוֹלָם חַסְדּוֹ:

Out of my straitness I called upon the Lord: the Lord answered me with enlargement. The Lord is for me, I will not fear: what can man do unto me? The Lord is for me among them that help me; therefore shall I see my desire on them that hate me. It is better to trust in the Lord than to confide in man. It is better to trust in the Lord than to confide in princes. All nations compassed me

מִן־הַמֵּצַר קָרָאתִי יָּהּ עָנָנִי בַמֶּרְחָב יָהּ: יְיָ לִי לֹא אִירָא מַה־יַּעֲשֶׂה לִי אָדָם: יְיָ לִי בְּעֹזְרָי וַאֲנִי אֶרְאֶה בְשֹׂנְאָי: טוֹב לַחֲסוֹת בַּיְיָ מִבְּטֹחַ בָּאָדָם: טוֹב לַחֲסוֹת בַּיְיָ מִבְּטֹחַ

about: in the Name of the Lord I surely cut them down. They compassed me about; yea, they compassed me about: in the Name of the Lord I surely cut them down. They compassed me about like bees — they were extinguished as a fire of thorns — in the Name of the Lord I surely cut them down. Thou didst thrust sore at me that I might fall: but the Lord helped me. The Lord is my strength and song; and he is become my salvation. The voice of exulting and salvation is in the tents of the righteous: the right hand of the Lord doeth valiantly. The right hand of the Lord is exalted: the right hand of the Lord doeth valiantly. I shall not die but live, and recount the works of the Lord. The Lord hath chastened me sore: but He hath not given me over unto death. Open to me the gates of righteousness: I will enter into them, I will give thanks unto the Lord. This is the gate of the Lord: the righteous may enter into it.

בְּנְדִיבִים: כָּל־גּוֹיִם סְבָבוּנִי בְּשֵׁם יְיָ כִּי

אֲמִילַם: סַבּוּנִי גַם־סְבָבוּנִי בְּשֵׁם יְיָ כִּי

אֲמִילַם: סַבּוּנִי כִדְבֹרִים דֹּעֲכוּ כְּאֵשׁ

קוֹצִים בְּשֵׁם יְיָ כִּי אֲמִילַם: דָּחֹה דְחִיתַנִי

לִנְפֹּל וַיְיָ עֲזָרָנִי: עָזִּי וְזִמְרָת יָהּ וַיְהִי־לִי

לִישׁוּעָה: קוֹל רִנָּה וִישׁוּעָה בְּאָהֳלֵי

צַדִּיקִים יְמִין יְיָ עֹשָׂה חָיִל: יְמִין יְיָ רוֹמֵמָה

יְמִין יְיָ עֹשָׂה חָיִל: לֹא־אָמוּת כִּי־אֶחְיֶה

וַאֲסַפֵּר מַעֲשֵׂי יָהּ: יַסֹּר יִסְּרַנִּי יָּהּ וְלַמָּוֶת

לֹא נְתָנָנִי:

פִּתְחוּ־לִי שַׁעֲרֵי־צֶדֶק אָבֹא־בָם אוֹדֶה

יָהּ: זֶה־הַשַּׁעַר לַיְיָ צַדִּיקִים יָבֹאוּ בוֹ:

The following four verses are repeated:

I will give thanks unto Thee, for Thou hast answered unto me, and art become my salvation.

אוֹדְךָ כִּי עֲנִיתָנִי וַתְּהִי־לִי
לִישׁוּעָה:

The stone which the builders rejected is become the head-stone of the corner.

אֶבֶן מָאֲסוּ הַבּוֹנִים הָיְתָה
לְרֹאשׁ פִּנָּה:

This was the Lord's doing; it is marvellous in our eyes.

מֵאֵת יְיָ הָיְתָה זֹּאת הִיא
נִפְלָאת בְּעֵינֵינוּ:

This is the day which the Lord hath made; we will be glad and rejoice thereon.

זֶה־הַיּוֹם עָשָׂה יְיָ נָגִילָה
וְנִשְׂמְחָה בוֹ:

Save, we beseech Thee, O Lord:
> Save, we beseech Thee, O Lord.

We beseech Thee, O Lord, send prosperity:
> We beseech Thee, O Lord, send prosperity.

אָנָּא יְיָ הוֹשִׁיעָה נָּא ·

אָנָּא יְיָ הוֹשִׁיעָה נָּא :

אָנָּא יְיָ הַצְלִיחָה נָּא ·

אָנָּא יְיָ הַצְלִיחָה נָּא :

The following verses are repeated:

Blessed be he that cometh in the Name of the Lord: we bless you out of the house of the Lord.

בָּרוּךְ הַבָּא בְּשֵׁם יְיָ בֵּרַכְנוּכֶם מִבֵּית יְיָ :

The Lord is God, He hath given us light: bind the festal offerings with cords, even unto the horns of the altar.

אֵל יְיָ וַיָּאֶר לָנוּ אִסְרוּ־חַג בַּעֲבֹתִים עַד־קַרְנוֹת הַמִּזְבֵּחַ :

Thou art my God, and I will give thanks unto Thee: Thou art my God, I will exalt Thee.

אֵלִי אַתָּה וְאוֹדֶךָ אֱלֹהַי אֲרוֹמְמֶךָ :

O give thanks unto the Lord; for He is good: for His lovingkindness endureth for ever.

הוֹדוּ לַיְיָ כִּי־טוֹב כִּי לְעוֹלָם חַסְדּוֹ :

All Thy works shall praise Thee, O Lord, our God: and Thy pious ones, the just who do Thy will, and all the house of Israel shall thank and bless and praise and glorify and exalt and reverence and sanctify and ascribe sovereignty to Thy Name, O our King, in song. For it is good to give thanks unto Thee, and becoming to sing praises to Thy Name: for from everlasting unto everlasting Thou art God.

יְהַלְלוּךָ יְיָ אֱלֹהֵינוּ כָּל־מַעֲשֶׂיךָ · וַחֲסִידֶיךָ צַדִּיקִים עוֹשֵׂי רְצוֹנֶךָ · וְכָל־עַמְּךָ בֵּית־יִשְׂרָאֵל בְּרִנָּה יוֹדוּ וִיבָרְכוּ וִישַׁבְּחוּ וִיפָאֲרוּ וִירוֹמְמוּ וְיַעֲרִיצוּ וְיַקְדִּישׁוּ וְיַמְלִיכוּ אֶת שִׁמְךָ מַלְכֵּנוּ : כִּי לְךָ טוֹב לְהוֹדוֹת · וּלְשִׁמְךָ נָאֶה לְזַמֵּר · כִּי מֵעוֹלָם וְעַד־עוֹלָם אַתָּה אֵל :

59

Ps. cxxxvi. O give thanks unto the Lord; for He is good:
    for His lovingkindness endureth for ever.

הוֹדוּ לַיְיָ כִּי־טוֹב
כִּי לְעוֹלָם חַסְדּוֹ:

O give thanks unto the God of gods:
    for His lovingkindness endureth for ever.

הוֹדוּ לֵאלֹהֵי הָאֱלֹהִים
כִּי לְעוֹלָם חַסְדּוֹ:

O give thanks unto the Lord of lords:
    for His lovingkindness endureth for ever.

הוֹדוּ לַאֲדֹנֵי הָאֲדֹנִים
כִּי לְעוֹלָם חַסְדּוֹ:

To Him who alone doeth great marvels:
    for His lovingkindness endureth for ever.

לְעֹשֵׂה נִפְלָאוֹת גְּדוֹלוֹת לְבַדּוֹ
כִּי לְעוֹלָם חַסְדּוֹ:

To Him that by understanding made the heavens:
    for His lovingkindness endureth for ever.

לְעֹשֵׂה הַשָּׁמַיִם בִּתְבוּנָה
כִּי לְעוֹלָם חַסְדּוֹ:

To Him that spread forth the earth above the waters:
    for His lovingkindness endureth for ever.

לְרוֹקַע הָאָרֶץ עַל־הַמָּיִם
כִּי לְעוֹלָם חַסְדּוֹ:

To Him that made great lights:
    for His lovingkindness endureth for ever.

לְעֹשֵׂה אוֹרִים גְּדֹלִים
כִּי לְעוֹלָם חַסְדּוֹ:

The sun to rule by day:
    for His lovingkindness endureth for ever.

אֶת־הַשֶּׁמֶשׁ לְמֶמְשֶׁלֶת בַּיּוֹם
כִּי לְעוֹלָם חַסְדּוֹ:

The moon and the stars to rule by night:
    for His lovingkindness endureth for ever.

אֶת־הַיָּרֵחַ וְכוֹכָבִים לְמֶמְשְׁלוֹת
בַּלָּיְלָה   כִּי לְעוֹלָם חַסְדּוֹ:

To Him that smote the Egyptians in their first-born: for His lovingkindness endureth for ever.

לְמַכֵּה מִצְרַיִם בִּבְכוֹרֵיהֶם
כִּי לְעוֹלָם חַסְדּוֹ:

And brought out Israel from among them: for His lovingkindness endureth for ever.

וַיּוֹצֵא יִשְׂרָאֵל מִתּוֹכָם
כִּי לְעוֹלָם חַסְדּוֹ:

With a strong hand and a stretched out arm: for His lovingkindness endureth for ever.

בְּיָד חֲזָקָה וּבִזְרוֹעַ נְטוּיָה
כִּי לְעוֹלָם חַסְדּוֹ:

To Him who parted the Red Sea in sunder: for His lovingkindness endureth for ever.

לְגֹזֵר יַם־סוּף לִגְזָרִים
כִּי לְעוֹלָם חַסְדּוֹ:

And made Israel to pass through the midst of it: for His lovingkindness endureth for ever.

וְהֶעֱבִיר יִשְׂרָאֵל בְּתוֹכוֹ
כִּי לְעוֹלָם חַסְדּוֹ:

But overthrew Pharaoh and his host in the Red Sea: for His lovingkindness endureth for ever.

וְנִעֵר פַּרְעֹה וְחֵילוֹ בְיַם־סוּף
כִּי לְעוֹלָם חַסְדּוֹ:

To Him who led his people through the wilderness: for His lovingkindness endureth for ever.

לְמוֹלִיךְ עַמּוֹ בַּמִּדְבָּר
כִּי לְעוֹלָם חַסְדּוֹ:

To Him who smote great kings: for His lovingkindness endureth for ever.

לְמַכֵּה מְלָכִים גְּדוֹלִים
כִּי לְעוֹלָם חַסְדּוֹ:

And slew mighty kings: for His lovingkindness endureth for ever.

וַיַּהֲרֹג מְלָכִים אַדִּירִים
כִּי לְעוֹלָם חַסְדּוֹ:

61

Sihon king of the Amorites:
    for His lovingkindness
      endureth for ever.

לְסִיחוֹן מֶלֶךְ הָאֱמֹרִי
כִּי לְעוֹלָם חַסְדּוֹ:

And Og king of Bashan:
    for His lovingkindness
      endureth for ever.

וּלְעוֹג מֶלֶךְ הַבָּשָׁן
כִּי לְעוֹלָם חַסְדּוֹ:

And gave their land for an
heritage:
    for His lovingkindness
      endureth for ever.

וְנָתַן אַרְצָם לְנַחֲלָה
כִּי לְעוֹלָם חַסְדּוֹ:

Even an heritage unto Israel
his servant:
    for His lovingkindness
      endureth for ever.

נַחֲלָה לְיִשְׂרָאֵל עַבְדּוֹ
כִּי לְעוֹלָם חַסְדּוֹ:

Who remembered us in our
low estate:
    for His lovingkindness
      endureth for ever.

שֶׁבְּשִׁפְלֵנוּ זָכַר לָנוּ
כִּי לְעוֹלָם חַסְדּוֹ:

And hath released us from
our adversaries:
    for His lovingkindness
      endureth for ever.

וַיִּפְרְקֵנוּ מִצָּרֵינוּ
כִּי לְעוֹלָם חַסְדּוֹ:

He giveth food to all flesh:
    for His lovingkindness
      endureth for ever.

נֹתֵן לֶחֶם לְכָל־בָּשָׂר
כִּי לְעוֹלָם חַסְדּוֹ:

O give thanks unto the God
of heaven:
    for His lovingkindness
      endureth for ever.

הוֹדוּ לְאֵל הַשָּׁמָיִם
כִּי לְעוֹלָם חַסְדּוֹ:

The breath of all that lives shall praise Thy Name, O Lord, our God, and the spirit of all flesh shall glorify and exalt Thy remembrance, O our King. Continually, from everlasting to everlasting, Thou art God, and beside Thee we have no King who redeemeth and saveth, delivereth and protecteth, sustaineth and pitieth in all time of trouble and stress: we have no King but Thee. Thou art God of the first and of the last: God of all creatures, Lord of all generations, who is lauded with many praises, and who guideth His world with lovingkindness and His creatures with mercy. For the Lord neither slumbereth nor sleepeth: He awakeneth those that sleep and arouseth those that slumber, giveth

נִשְׁמַת כָּל־חַי תְּבָרֵךְ אֶת־
שְׁמְךָ יְיָ אֱלֹהֵינוּ · וְרוּחַ כָּל־
בָּשָׂר תְּפָאֵר וּתְרוֹמֵם זִכְרְךָ
מַלְכֵּנוּ תָּמִיד · מִן־הָעוֹלָם עַד־
הָעוֹלָם אַתָּה אֵל · וּמִבַּלְעָדֶיךָ
אֵין לָנוּ מֶלֶךְ גּוֹאֵל וּמוֹשִׁיעַ
פּוֹדֶה וּמַצִּיל וּמְפַרְנֵס וּמְרַחֵם
בְּכָל־עֵת צָרָה וְצוּקָה אֵין־לָנוּ
מֶלֶךְ אֶלָּא אָתָּה: אֱלֹהֵי
הָרִאשׁוֹנִים וְהָאַחֲרוֹנִים · אֱלוֹהַּ
כָּל־בְּרִיּוֹת אֲדוֹן כָּל־תּוֹלָדוֹת ·
הַמְהֻלָּל בְּרֹב הַתִּשְׁבָּחוֹת ·
הַמְנַהֵג עוֹלָמוֹ בְּחֶסֶד וּבְרִיּוֹתָיו
בְּרַחֲמִים · וַיְיָ לֹא־יָנוּם וְלֹא־
יִישָׁן: הַמְעוֹרֵר יְשֵׁנִים וְהַמֵּקִיץ

נשמת The Nishmat prayer (referred to in the Talmud (T. B. Pes. 118a) as the 'Blessing of Song' prescribed for recital at the close of the *Haggadah*) is one of the finest specimens of the post-Biblical revival of Hebrew literature. More than one reference to it occurs in the Talmud: and it seems probable that its main elements at least date back to the second century. Part of it, perhaps, grew out of the earliest prayer for rain (T. B. Ber. 59b), in connection with which it is once cited. It is now recited on the morning of every Sabbath and festival after the reading of the selected psalms of the day, in much the same relative position as that in which it figures here. A remarkable mediæval legend is, however, connected with it — perhaps the most remarkable in the whole range of Jewish folk-lore. It is said that a certain Simeon Caipha (the latter name is the Aramaic equivalent for the Greek 'Peter') was filled with alarm at the disruption which the teachings of Christianity were causing in the ranks of Judaism. Accordingly, he feigned adherence to the new sect and used his influence to bring about a definite breach with the parent religion, which would gain rather than lose by the loss of this discordant offshoot. In this policy he achieved a complete success. Henceforth he was known as Peter, since he absolved (Hebrew P T R) his followers from their allegiance to the Torah. Having established the headquarters of the new faith at Rome, he shut himself up there in a tower, where he compiled the Nishmat prayer for the adherents of the old religion, to which he remained faithful at heart.

speech to the dumb, loos-
eneth the bound, supporteth
the falling, and raiseth up the
bowed. To Thee alone do
we give thanks.

Even though our mouths
were filled with song as the
sea, and our tongues with joy
as its multitude of waves,
and our lips with praise as
the expanse of the firma-
ment: though our eyes were
radiant as the sun and the
moon, and our hands were
outspread as the wings of the
eagles of heaven, and our
feet were fleet as the hinds':
we should yet be inadequate
to thank Thee, O Lord, our
God, and God of our Fa-
thers, for one in a thousand
of the many thousands of
thousands and myriads of
myriads of lovingkindnesses
that Thou hast bestowed
on our fathers and on us.

From Egypt didst Thou de-
liver us, O Lord, our God,
and from the house of bondage didst Thou release us: in
famine didst Thou feed us,
and in plenty didst Thou
sustain us: from the sword
didst Thou deliver us, and
from pestilence didst Thou
protect us, and from sore and
grievous sickness didst Thou
withdraw us. Thus far Thy
mercies have helped us, and

d

נִרְדָּמִים וְהַמֵּשִׂיחַ אִלְּמִים
וְהַמַּתִּיר אֲסוּרִים וְהַסּוֹמֵךְ
נוֹפְלִים וְהַזּוֹקֵף כְּפוּפִים · לְךָ
לְבַדְּךָ אֲנַחְנוּ מוֹדִים : אִלּוּ
פִינוּ מָלֵא שִׁירָה כַּיָּם וּלְשׁוֹנֵנוּ
רִנָּה כַּהֲמוֹן גַּלָּיו וְשִׂפְתוֹתֵינוּ
שֶׁבַח כְּמֶרְחֲבֵי רָקִיעַ וְעֵינֵינוּ
מְאִירוֹת כַּשֶּׁמֶשׁ וְכַיָּרֵחַ וְיָדֵינוּ
פְרוּשׂוֹת כְּנִשְׁרֵי שָׁמַיִם וְרַגְלֵינוּ
קַלּוֹת כָּאַיָּלוֹת · אֵין אֲנַחְנוּ
מַסְפִּיקִים לְהוֹדוֹת לְךָ יְיָ אֱלֹהֵינוּ
וֵאלֹהֵי אֲבוֹתֵינוּ וּלְבָרֵךְ אֶת־
שְׁמֶךָ עַל־אַחַת מֵאָלֶף אֶלֶף
אַלְפֵי אֲלָפִים וְרִבֵּי רְבָבוֹת
פְּעָמִים הַטּוֹבוֹת שֶׁעָשִׂיתָ עִם־
אֲבוֹתֵינוּ וְעִמָּנוּ : מִמִּצְרַיִם
גְּאַלְתָּנוּ יְיָ אֱלֹהֵינוּ וּמִבֵּית
עֲבָדִים פְּדִיתָנוּ · בְּרָעָב זַנְתָּנוּ
וּבְשָׂבָע כִּלְכַּלְתָּנוּ · וּמֵחֶרֶב
הִצַּלְתָּנוּ וּמִדֶּבֶר מִלַּטְתָּנוּ ·
וּמֵחֳלָיִם רָעִים וְנֶאֱמָנִים
דִּלִּיתָנוּ : עַד־הֵנָּה עֲזָרוּנוּ
רַחֲמֶיךָ · וְלֹא־עֲזָבוּנוּ חֲסָדֶיךָ ·

64

Thy lovingkindnesses have not deserted us: O, forsake us not, O Lord, our God, for ever! Wherefore, the limbs which Thou hast formed in us, and the breath and spirit which Thou hast blown into our nostrils, and the tongue which Thou hast placed in our mouths — lo! they shall thank, bless, praise, glorify, extol, reverence, hallow, and ascribe sovereignty to Thy Name, O our King!

For to Thee every mouth shall give thanks, to Thee every tongue shall swear, to Thee every knee shall bend, and before Thee every stature shall bow down: Thee every heart shall fear, and unto Thy Name shall all men's inmost being sing praise; according to that which is written:

'All my bones shall say: O Lord, who is like unto Thee? which delivereth the poor from him that is too strong for him, yea, the poor and the needy from him that spoileth him?' (Ps. xxxv. 10)

Who is like unto Thee? who is equal to Thee? who can be compared unto Thee? Thou great, mighty, and tremendous God, most high God, possessor of heaven and earth! We will praise

65

וְאַל־תִּטְּשֵׁנוּ יְיָ אֱלֹהֵינוּ לָנֶצַח:
עַל־כֵּן אֵבָרִים שֶׁפִּלַּגְתָּ בָּנוּ
וְרוּחַ וּנְשָׁמָה שֶׁנָּפַחְתָּ בְּאַפֵּינוּ
וְלָשׁוֹן אֲשֶׁר שַׂמְתָּ בְּפִינוּ · הֵן
הֵם יוֹדוּ וִיבָרְכוּ וִישַׁבְּחוּ
וִיפָאֲרוּ וִירוֹמְמוּ וְיַעֲרִיצוּ
וְיַקְדִּישׁוּ וְיַמְלִיכוּ אֶת־שִׁמְךָ
מַלְכֵּנוּ: כִּי כָל־פֶּה לְךָ יוֹדֶה ·
וְכָל־לָשׁוֹן לְךָ תִשָּׁבַע · וְכָל־
בֶּרֶךְ לְךָ תִכְרַע · וְכָל־קוֹמָה
לְפָנֶיךָ תִשְׁתַּחֲוֶה · וְכָל־לְבָבוֹת
יִירָאוּךָ · וְכָל־קֶרֶב וּכְלָיוֹת
יְזַמְּרוּ לִשְׁמֶךָ · כַּדָּבָר שֶׁכָּתוּב ·
כָּל־עַצְמוֹתַי תֹּאמַרְנָה יְיָ מִי
כָמוֹךָ · מַצִּיל עָנִי מֵחָזָק מִמֶּנּוּ
וְעָנִי וְאֶבְיוֹן מִגֹּזְלוֹ: מִי יִדְמֶה
לָּךְ וּמִי יִשְׁוֶה־לָּךְ וּמִי יַעֲרָךְ־
לָּךְ · הָאֵל הַגָּדוֹל הַגִּבּוֹר
וְהַנּוֹרָא אֵל עֶלְיוֹן קֹנֵה שָׁמַיִם
וָאָרֶץ: נְהַלֶּלְךָ וּנְשַׁבֵּחֲךָ
וּנְפָאֶרְךָ וּנְבָרֵךְ אֶת־שֵׁם קָדְשֶׁךָ
כָּאָמוּר לְדָוִד בָּרְכִי נַפְשִׁי

Thee, laud Thee, glorify Thee, and bless Thy holy Name: as David said: 'Bless the Lord, O my soul; and all that is within me, bless His holy Name' (Ps. ciii. 1).

O God! in the might of Thy power, great in the glory of Thy Name, mighty for ever, tremendous by Thy tremendous acts! O King, who sitteth upon a high and lofty throne!

He that abideth eternally, exalted and holy is His Name. It is written: 'Rejoice in the Lord, O ye righteous, for praise is comely for the upright' (Ps. xxxiii. 1).

In the mouth of the upright shalt Thou be praised: with the words of the righteous shalt Thou be blessed: by the tongue of the pious shalt Thou be extolled: and in the inmost being of the holy shalt Thou be hallowed.

And in the assemblies of the multitudes of Thy people, the house of Israel, shall Thy Name be glorified in song, O our King, in every generation. For such is the duty of all creatures — before Thee, O Lord, our God, and God of our fathers, to thank, praise, laud, glorify, extol, reverence, bless, exalt and

אֶת־יְיָ. וְכָל־קְרָבַי אֶת־שֵׁם קָדְשׁוֹ:

הָאֵל בְּתַעֲצֻמוֹת עֻזֶּךָ: הַגָּדוֹל בִּכְבוֹד שְׁמֶךָ: הַגִּבּוֹר לָנֶצַח וְהַנּוֹרָא בְּנוֹרְאוֹתֶיךָ:

הַמֶּלֶךְ הַיּוֹשֵׁב עַל־כִּסֵּא רָם וְנִשָּׂא:

שׁוֹכֵן עַד מָרוֹם וְקָדוֹשׁ שְׁמוֹ: וְכָתוּב. רַנְּנוּ צַדִּיקִים בַּיְיָ לַיְשָׁרִים נָאוָה תְהִלָּה: בְּפִי יְשָׁרִים תִּתְהַלָּל. וּבְדִבְרֵי צַדִּיקִים תִּתְבָּרַךְ. וּבִלְשׁוֹן חֲסִידִים תִּתְרוֹמָם. וּבְקֶרֶב קְדוֹשִׁים תִּתְקַדָּשׁ:

וּבְמַקְהֲלוֹת רִבְבוֹת עַמְּךָ בֵּית יִשְׂרָאֵל בְּרִנָּה יִתְפָּאַר שִׁמְךָ מַלְכֵּנוּ בְּכָל־דּוֹר וָדוֹר: שֶׁכֵּן חוֹבַת כָּל־הַיְצוּרִים לְפָנֶיךָ יְיָ אֱלֹהֵינוּ וֵאלֹהֵי אֲבוֹתֵינוּ: לְהוֹדוֹת לְהַלֵּל לְשַׁבֵּחַ לְפָאֵר לְרוֹמֵם לְהַדֵּר לְבָרֵךְ לְעַלֵּה

adore, above all the words of the songs and praises of David the son of Jesse, Thine anointed servant.

Be Thy Name praised for ever, O our King: God and King, great and hallowed in Heaven and on earth. For unto Thee are becoming, O Lord, our God, and God of our fathers, song and praise, adoration and psalmody, strength and dominion: victory, greatness, and might; praise and glory; holiness and sovereignty; blessings and thanksgiving, from henceforth and for ever.

Blessed art Thou, O Lord, God and King, great in praises, God of thanksgivings, Lord of wonders, who delightest in songs of praise, King and God, Life of all worlds!

Blessed art Thou, O Lord, our God, King of the Universe, Creator of the fruit of the vine.

וּלְקַלֵּס עַל־כָּל־דִּבְרֵי שִׁירוֹת
וְתִשְׁבְּחוֹת דָּוִד בֶּן־יִשַׁי עַבְדְּךָ
מְשִׁיחֶךָ:

יִשְׁתַּבַּח שִׁמְךָ לָעַד מַלְכֵּנוּ
הָאֵל הַמֶּלֶךְ הַגָּדוֹל וְהַקָּדוֹשׁ
בַּשָּׁמַיִם וּבָאָרֶץ: כִּי־לְךָ נָאֶה
יְיָ אֱלֹהֵינוּ וֵאלֹהֵי אֲבוֹתֵינוּ שִׁיר
וּשְׁבָחָה הַלֵּל וְזִמְרָה עֹז
וּמֶמְשָׁלָה נֶצַח גְּדֻלָּה וּגְבוּרָה
תְּהִלָּה וְתִפְאֶרֶת קְדֻשָׁה
וּמַלְכוּת בְּרָכוֹת וְהוֹדָאוֹת
מֵעַתָּה וְעַד־עוֹלָם: בָּרוּךְ אַתָּה
יְיָ אֵל מֶלֶךְ גָּדוֹל בַּתִּשְׁבָּחוֹת.
אֵל הַהוֹדָאוֹת. אֲדוֹן הַנִּפְלָאוֹת.
הַבּוֹחֵר בְּשִׁירֵי זִמְרָה. מֶלֶךְ
אֵל חֵי הָעוֹלָמִים:

בָּרוּךְ אַתָּה יְיָ אֱלֹהֵינוּ מֶלֶךְ
הָעוֹלָם. בּוֹרֵא פְּרִי הַגָּפֶן:

The fourth, and last, cup of wine is drunk. The following Grace is then pronounced, the italicised words being added if it should be the Sabbath:

67

Blessed art Thou, O Lord, our God, King of the Universe, for the vine and for the fruit of the vine, and for the pleasant, goodly, and ample land which Thou didst please to give as an inheritance to our Fathers, to eat of its fruit and to be satisfied with its goodness. Have mercy, O Lord, our God, upon Israel Thy people and upon Jerusalem Thy city and upon Zion the abode of Thy glory and upon Thine altar and upon Thy shrine. Build Thou again Jerusalem the Holy City speedily in our days; bring us up into its midst and cause us to rejoice in its establishment, so that we may eat of its fruit and be satisfied with its goodness and bless Thee for it in holiness and purity: *Be pleased to strengthen us upon this Sabbath day,* and make us to rejoice upon this Feast of Unleavened Bread. For Thou, O Lord, art good, and doest good to all: and we shall thank Thee for the Land and for the fruit of the Vine. Blessed art Thou, O Lord, for the Land and for the fruit of the Vine!

בָּרוּךְ אַתָּה יְיָ אֱלֹהֵינוּ מֶלֶךְ הָעוֹלָם. עַל־הַגֶּפֶן וְעַל־פְּרִי הַגֶּפֶן. וְעַל תְּנוּבַת הַשָּׂדֶה וְעַל־אֶרֶץ חֶמְדָּה טוֹבָה וּרְחָבָה שֶׁרָצִיתָ וְהִנְחַלְתָּ לַאֲבוֹתֵינוּ לֶאֱכֹל מִפִּרְיָהּ וְלִשְׂבֹּעַ מִטּוּבָהּ: רַחֵם יְיָ אֱלֹהֵינוּ עַל־יִשְׂרָאֵל עַמֶּךָ וְעַל־יְרוּשָׁלַיִם עִירֶךָ. וְעַל־צִיּוֹן מִשְׁכַּן כְּבוֹדֶךָ. וְעַל־מִזְבְּחֶךָ וְעַל־הֵיכָלֶךָ. וּבְנֵה יְרוּשָׁלַיִם עִיר הַקֹּדֶשׁ בִּמְהֵרָה בְיָמֵינוּ. וְהַעֲלֵנוּ לְתוֹכָהּ וְשַׂמְּחֵנוּ בְּבִנְיָנָהּ. וְנֹאכַל מִפִּרְיָהּ וְנִשְׂבַּע מִטּוּבָהּ. וּנְבָרֶכְךָ עָלֶיהָ בִּקְדֻשָּׁה וּבְטָהֳרָה: [וּרְצֵה וְהַחֲלִיצֵנוּ בְּיוֹם הַשַּׁבָּת הַזֶּה] וְשַׂמְּחֵנוּ בְּיוֹם חַג הַמַּצּוֹת הַזֶּה. כִּי־אַתָּה יְיָ טוֹב וּמֵטִיב לַכֹּל וְנוֹדֶה לְּךָ עַל הָאָרֶץ וְעַל פְּרִי הַגֶּפֶן: בָּרוּךְ אַתָּה יְיָ עַל הָאָרֶץ וְעַל פְּרִי הַגֶּפֶן:

ENVOI

Accomplished is the order of the Passover according to its precept, to all its law and its custom.
Even as we have had the merit to order it,
So may we have the merit to fulfil it.
Thou Pure One, who dwellest on high!
Redress the congregation that is without number!
Speedily lead Thou the offshoots of the stock Thou hast planted,
Redeemed, to Zion in song.

נִרְצָה

חֲסַל סִדּוּר פֶּסַח כְּהִלְכָתוֹ. כְּכָל־מִשְׁפָּטוֹ וְחֻקָּתוֹ: כַּאֲשֶׁר זָכִינוּ לְסַדֵּר אוֹתוֹ. כֵּן נִזְכֶּה לַעֲשׂוֹתוֹ: זָךְ שׁוֹכֵן מְעוֹנָה. קוֹמֵם קְהַל מִי מָנָה: בְּקָרוֹב נַהֵל נִטְעֵי כַנָּה. פְּדוּיִם לְצִיּוֹן בְּרִנָּה:

NEXT YEAR
IN JERUSALEM

לְשָׁנָה הַבָּאָה
בִּירוּשָׁלָיִם:

THE HYMNS

ENVOI: The drinking of the last cup of wine, over which the Thanksgiving has been recited, and the repetition of the appropriate Grace has ended the essential and the universal part of the Seder Service. It is rounded off, according to the Ashkenazic rite, by the charming poem just read. This forms the concluding passage of a detailed account of the laws of Passover in rhyme recited in the synagogues on the previous Sabbath. The author was Rabbi Joseph Bonfils (Tob-Elem), a Provençal scholar of the eleventh century. So great was his repute that his poem was considered a standard guide for conduct. It is often cited with the deference due to an authoritative work, and has even formed the subject of a formal commentary. Here it serves (in the Ashkenazic rite alone) as the *envoi* to the *Haggadah* proper, being succeeded by a prayer of three words, that the next year might witness the celebration of the observance in Jerusalem. With the terse expression of this eternal hope, the essential part of the ceremonial of the evening ends. The word here rendered 'envoi' means literally *Accepted!*

THE CONCLUSION OF THE SERVICE: The statutory part of the *Haggadah* is now ended. Indeed, the Spanish rite concludes the whole service with the Grace after wine. It early became customary, however, to add a number of hymns: first, perhaps, a voluntary choice, but ultimately more definitely fixed. The selection varied from country to country. In mediæval France, according to the Mahzor Vitry, the hymn, 'The loved ones sang in joy and gladness', by Isaac ben Samuel, was recited. The Byzantine rite interpolated 'May He who wrought judgement in Egypt so also wreak judgement on the Foe'. According to the rite of Avignon, two mystical hymns, one based on the Song of Songs, are included. Our Ashkenazic rite has the richest selection of all. A formal hymn (alternatives being given for the first and second night) begins the series. This is succeeded by a succession of religious folk-songs of extraordinary interest, intended without doubt to appeal to the children, whose night above all this was reckoned.

THE OPENING HYMNS: The alternative opening hymns are very much the same in nature and style, being intended to show the importance of the Passover in all generations, past and future. Both are allusive in the extreme, and demand a profound knowledge of Biblical and Talmudic lore to be appreciated to the full. Scriptural phrases are quoted at every turn, but, when once the crudity and intricacy of expression are penetrated, both reveal themselves as poems of extraordinary force, if not of extraordinary beauty. Both in their force and in their crudities these hymns are, as a matter of fact, valuable specimens of the earliest stage of mediæval Hebrew poetry. The first, which is to be found also in the liturgy of the Sabbath preceding the Passover, is in all probability by Yannai, who flourished in Palestine in the first half of the seventh century: the earliest Hebrew poet to employ rhyme and to introduce his name in his acrostical forms (the alternative ascription to Joseph Tob-Elem, a specimen of whose work we have seen above, is most improbable). The poem is based upon the Midrash Rabba on Exodus, Chapter xviii, in which are collected the various miracles which occurred to the Hebrews and to their ancestors 'at night'—in some cases on the Passover night, which was considered the night *par excellence*. This leads up to an allusion to the hoped-for redemption, which is also, according to tradition, to take place on this night.

The second poem is by Yannai's legendary pupil and rival, Kalir, the real father of neo-Hebrew poetry. In this, by similar means, references are collected to the Passover. If this was 'a night of guarding for the children of Israel in all their generations', more than the single deliverance from Egypt must be associated with the anniversary. Accordingly, by a microscopic examination of the Biblical text, the Rabbis found reason for believing that a number of other miraculous deliverances, both before and after, are to be associated with this same season of the year. Thus, every time when reference is made to the preparation of unleavened bread (in the old days, the invariable emergency fare), the event must necessarily have taken place in the Passover season. It is these references which Kalir has collected in the second poem, making them lead up, as in the previous case, to the hoped-for deliverance traditionally associated with this festival.

It will be noticed that, in both of these poems, the acrostical order is followed: that is to say, each stanza begins with a successive letter of the Hebrew alphabet. This method (of which traces are found, not infrequently, even in the Bible) was the almost invariable practice in mediæval Hebrew poetry: and it is remarkable to see how ably some poets are able to free themselves from these awkward shackles. It must not be imagined, however, that this was a mere artificial convention, with no object other than to display the skill of the poet. In the old days, before the invention of printing, books were rare and expensive in the extreme. Memory played accordingly a much more important part than it does to-day. To remember the more usual prayers, recited every day, was none too difficult. But occasional poems were not so familiar, and confusion might easily take place. By introducing an alphabetical acrostic into their compositions, the mediæval hymnologists rendered it much more easy for their compositions to be remembered and for the stanzas to be repeated in the proper order.

For the First Night:

AND IT HAPPENED AT THE MIDDLE OF THE NIGHT
(Ex. xii. 29)

וַיְהִי בַּחֲצִי הַלַּיְלָה:

Of old, Thou didst perform most miracles at night,

At the beginning of the watches of this night.

The righteous proselyte prevailed when he broke up his host at night. (Gen. xiv. 15)

And it happened at the middle of the night.

אָז רוֹב נִסִּים הִפְלֵאתָ בַּלַּיְלָה.
בְּרֹאשׁ אַשְׁמוֹרֶת זֶה הַלַּיְלָה.
גֵּר צֶדֶק נִצַּחְתּוֹ כְּנֶחֱלַק לוֹ לַיְלָה.
וַיְהִי בַּחֲצִי הַלַּיְלָה:

Thou didst judge the king of Gerar in a dream of night, (Gen. xx. 3)

The Syrian was struck with terror 'yesternight', (Gen. xxxi. 24)

And Israel strove with God, and yet prevailed at night. (Gen. xxxii. 23-7)

And it happened at the middle of the night.

דַּנְתָּ מֶלֶךְ גְּרָר בַּחֲלוֹם הַלַּיְלָה.
הִפְחַדְתָּ אֲרַמִּי בְּאֶמֶשׁ לָיְלָה.
וַיִּשַֹר יִשְׂרָאֵל לְאֵל וַיּוּכַל לוֹ לָיְלָה.
וַיְהִי בַּחֲצִי הַלַּיְלָה:

The first-born seed of Pathros didst thou crush in dead of night. (Ex. xii. 29)

Their substance they found not when they rose at night.

The battalions of Harosheth's captain didst sweep away through the stars of night. (Jud. v. 20)

And it happened at the middle of the night.

זֶרַע בְּכוֹרֵי פַתְרוֹס מָחַצְתָּ בַּחֲצִי הַלַּיְלָה.
חֵילָם לֹא מָצְאוּ בְּקוּמָם בַּלַּיְלָה.
טִיסַת נְגִיד חֲרֹשֶׁת סִלִּיתָ בְּכוֹכְבֵי לָיְלָה.
וַיְהִי בַּחֲצִי הַלַּיְלָה:

71

The impious thought to scatter My
chosen. Thou didst shame his dead
by night. (II Kings xix. 35)
Bel and his pillar were prostrate at night.
(Dan. ii. 34)
The man of delight was told the key of
mysteries of night. (Dan. ii. 19)
*And it happened at the middle of
the night.*

יָעַץ מְחָרֵף לְנוֹפֵף אִוּוּי הוֹבַשְׁתָּ פְגָרָיו
בַּלַּיְלָה.
כָּרַע בֵּל וּמַצָּבוֹ בְּאִישׁוֹן לַיְלָה.
לְאִישׁ חֲמוּדוֹת נִגְלָה רָז חֲזוֹת לַיְלָה.
וַיְהִי בַּחֲצִי הַלַּיְלָה:

He who was drunken in the sacred
vessels — he was slain that night,
When he who had escaped the lions' den
revealed the awesome dreams of night.
(Dan. v. 30)
The Agagite cherished hatred, and mis-
sives wrote at night. (Est. iv. 12)
*And it happened at the middle of
the night.*

מִשְׁתַּכֵּר בִּכְלֵי קֹדֶשׁ נֶהֱרַג בּוֹ בַּלַּיְלָה.
נוֹשַׁע מִבּוֹר אֲרָיוֹת פּוֹתֵר בְּעָתוּתֵי לַיְלָה.
שִׂנְאָה נָטַר אֲגָגִי וְכָתַב סְפָרִים בַּלַּיְלָה.
וַיְהִי בַּחֲצִי הַלַּיְלָה:

Thou didst arouse Thy victory on him,
when sleep fled at night. (Est. vi. 1)
The wine-press Thou shalt tread for him
who asks the watchman, What of
night? (Is. lxiii. 3; xxi. 11)
Like a watchman shall He answer,
saying: 'Morning's come, and, too,
the night.'
*And it happened at the middle of
the night.*

עוֹרַרְתָּ נִצְחֲךָ עָלָיו בְּנֶדֶד שְׁנַת־לַיְלָה.
פּוּרָה תִדְרוֹךְ לְשׁוֹמֵר מַה־מִלַּיְלָה.
צָרַח כַּשׁוֹמֵר וְשָׂח אָתָא בֹקֶר וְגַם־לָיְלָ
וַיְהִי בַּחֲצִי הַלַּיְלָה:

Bring near the day, which is not day nor
night!
All-High! Make known that Thine is
day and Thine is night!
Set guards about Thy city, all the day
and all the night:
Make Thou light as the day the dark of
night!
*And it happened at the middle of
the night.*

קָרֵב יוֹם אֲשֶׁר הוּא לֹא יוֹם וְלֹא לַיְלָה.
רָם הוֹדַע כִּי־לְךָ יוֹם אַף־לְךָ הַלַּיְלָה.
שׁוֹמְרִים הַפְקֵד לְעִירְךָ כָּל־הַיּוֹם וְכָל־
הַלַּיְלָה.
תָּאִיר כְּאוֹר יוֹם חֶשְׁכַת לַיְ,,,
וַיְהִי בַּחֲצִי הַלַּיְלָה:

AND YE SHALL SAY, 'TIS THE OFFERING OF THE PASSOVER.
(Ex. xii. 42)

וַאֲמַרְתֶּם זֶבַח־פֶּסַח:

The strength of Thy might was wondrously displayed on Passover:
Above all feasts didst Thou raise up the Passover:
To the Ezrahite Thou didst reveal the midnight marvels of the Passover. (Ps. LXXXIX. I)
And ye shall say, 'Tis the offering of the Passover.

אֹמֶץ גְּבוּרוֹתֶיךָ הִפְלֵאתָ בַּפֶּסַח.
בְּרֹאשׁ כָּל־מוֹעֲדוֹת נִשֵּׂאתָ פֶּסַח.
גִּלִּיתָ לְאֶזְרָחִי חֲצוֹת לֵיל פֶּסַח.
וַאֲמַרְתֶּם זֶבַח־פֶּסַח:

Upon his doors didst knock at noon-tide heat on Passover:
He feasted angels with unleavened cakes on Passover: (GEN. XVIII)
'And to the herd he ran': so do we read the Lesson of the Ox on Passover. (LEV. XXII. 26—XXIII. 44)
And ye shall say, 'Tis the offering of the Passover.

דְּלָתָיו דָּפַקְתָּ כְּחֹם הַיּוֹם בַּפֶּסַח.
הִסְעִיד נוֹצְצִים עֻגוֹת מַצּוֹת בַּפֶּסַח.
וְאֶל־הַבָּקָר רָץ זֵכֶר לְשׁוֹר עֵרֶךְ פֶּסַח.
וַאֲמַרְתֶּם זֶבַח־פֶּסַח:

The furious Sodomites Thou didst consume in fire on Passover:
Lot, saved from them, baked unleavened bread towards the end of Passover: (GEN. XIX)
Thou didst sweep clean the land of Moph and Noph when Thou didst near on Passover.
And ye shall say, 'Tis the offering of the Passover.

זוֹעֲמוּ סְדוֹמִים וְלוֹהֲטוּ בָּאֵשׁ בַּפֶּסַח.
חֻלַּץ לוֹט מֵהֶם וּמַצּוֹת אָפָה בְּקֵץ פֶּסַח.
טִאטֵאתָ אַדְמַת מוֹף וְנוֹף בְּעָבְרְךָ בַּפֶּסַח.
וַאֲמַרְתֶּם זֶבַח־פֶּסַח:

Lord! Thou didst smite each first-born's head on Passover:
Omnipotent! Thy first-born didst Thou spare on Passover:
Not suffering a destroyer to pass my doors on Passover. (Ex. XII)
And ye shall say, 'Tis the offering of the Passover.

יָהּ רֹאשׁ כָּל־אוֹן מָחַצְתָּ בְּלֵיל שִׁמּוּר פֶּסַח.
כַּבִּיר עַל־בֵּן־בְּכוֹר פָּסַחְתָּ בְּדַם־פֶּסַח.
לְבִלְתִּי תֵּת מַשְׁחִית לָבֹא בִּפְתָחַי בַּפֶּסַח.
וַאֲמַרְתֶּם זֶבַח־פֶּסַח:

73

Strong Jericho was straitly closed to-
wards the time of Passover: (JOSH. VI)
Midian was destroyed by a cake of bar-
ley, the offering of the Passover:
(JUD. VII)
The mighty ones of Pul and Lud were
burned up in a conflagration on the
Passover. (IS. LXVI. 19)
*And ye shall say, 'Tis the offering of
the Passover.*

מְסֻגֶּרֶת סֻגָּרָה בְּעִתּוֹתֵי פֶסַח .
נִשְׁמְדָה מִדְיָן בִּצְלִיל שְׂעוֹרֵי עוֹמֶר פֶסַח .
שׂוֹרְפוּ מִשְׁמַנֵּי פוּל וְלוּד בִּיקַד יְקוֹד פֶסַח .
וַאֲמַרְתֶּם זֶבַח־פֶּסַח :

Destined was he to stay in Nob, until
there came the time of Passover:
(IS. X. 32)
A Hand wrote Babylon's fate upon the
wall on Passover: (DAN. V. 24)
'The watch is set: the table spread'— on
Passover. (IS. XXI. 5)
*And ye shall say, 'Tis the offering of
the Passover.*

עוֹד הַיּוֹם בְּנֹב לַעֲמוֹד עַד גָּעָה עוֹנַת פֶסַח .
פַּס יָד כָּתְבָה לְקַעֲקֵעַ צוּל בְּפֶסַח .
צָפֹה הַצָּפִית עָרוֹךְ הַשֻּׁלְחָן בְּפֶסַח .
וַאֲמַרְתֶּם זֶבַח־פֶּסַח :

Hadassah gathered all, for three-fold fast
on Passover: (EST. IV. 16)
Thou didst smite the chief of the evil
house on Passover: (EST. VII. 9)
'These twain' shalt Thou together bring
for Edom on the Passover:(IS.XLVII.9)
Thy hand shall be strong: Thy right arm
uplifted as on the night of sanctification of the Passover.
*And ye shall say, 'Tis the offering of
the Passover.*

קָהָל כִּנְּסָה הֲדַסָּה לְשַׁלֵּשׁ צוֹם בְּפֶסַח .
רֹאשׁ מִבֵּית רָשָׁע מָחַצְתָּ בְּעֵץ חֲמִשִּׁים
בְּפֶסַח .
שְׁתֵּי אֵלֶּה רֶגַע תָּבִיא לְעוּצִית בְּפֶסַח .
תָּעֹז יָדְךָ תָּרוּם יְמִינְךָ כְּלֵיל הִתְקַדֶּשׁ חַג
פֶסַח .
וַאֲמַרְתֶּם זֶבַח־פֶּסַח :

TO HIM IS IT BECOMING, TO HIM SHALL IT BECOME!

כִּי לוֹ נָאֶה ּ כִּי לוֹ יָאֶה:

Mighty in kingship, Chosen
  of right!
To Him say His armies:
'To Thee, and to Thee,
To Thee, yea, to Thee,
To Thee, true, to Thee,
To Thee, Lord, is the sover-
  eignty:
To Him is it becoming,
To Him shall it become!'

אַדִּיר בִּמְלוּכָה ּ בָּחוּר
כַּהֲלָכָה ּ גְּדוּדָיו יֹאמְרוּ לוֹ ּ
לְךָ וּלְךָ ּ לְךָ כִּי לְךָ ּ לְךָ אַף
לְךָ ּ לְךָ יְיָ הַמַּמְלָכָה ּ כִּי לוֹ
נָאֶה ּ כִּי לוֹ יָאֶה:

Foremost in kingship, Glori-
  ous of right!
To Him say His trusty:
'To Thee, and to Thee,
To Thee, yea,'to Thee,
To Thee, true, to Thee,
To Thee, Lord, is the sover-
  eignty:
To Him is it becoming,
To Him shall it become!'

דָּגוּל בִּמְלוּכָה ּ הָדוּר
כַּהֲלָכָה ּ וָתִיקָיו יֹאמְרוּ לוֹ ּ
לְךָ וּלְךָ ּ לְךָ כִּי לְךָ ּ לְךָ אַף
לְךָ ּ לְךָ יְיָ הַמַּמְלָכָה ּ כִּי לוֹ
נָאֶה ּ כִּי לוֹ יָאֶה:

כי לו נאה: The date of the hymn which now follows is obscure. It is, however, the first of the folk-poems in the *Haggadah*; and its form makes it probable that it is a product of France or Germany, in the Middle Ages. The inspiration seems to derive from a passage in the Midrash (Genesis Rabba, § x). Originally, it may have been intended that this hymn should be recited on the first night, and that which follows (which resembles it closely in structure and probably in date) on the second. Such, however, is their popularity that both are now chanted on each occasion.

The language of the hymn is terse in the extreme: and the frequent repetitions have caused a considerable amount of speculation. It has accordingly been suggested that what we have here in the chorus is no more than the catchwords. Originally, according to this theory, the poem read '*To Thee* — is praise befitting by day: *and to Thee* — is it befitting by night', or some such formula. This was subsequently expressed in writing by the initial words, which were later assumed erroneously to constitute the whole poem. But this explanation, ingenious though it is, is wholly superfluous. The hymn, in its present form, is a fine example of the mediæval folk-hymn, which can be sung with a splendid swing: and to examine its structure too closely is to misunderstand its whole significance. As in the hymn which follows, ADDIR HU (which exists also in a curious Old German version), the various epithets used follow the alphabetical order.

75

All-pure in kingship, Power-
ful of right!
To Him say His courtiers:
'To Thee, and to Thee,
To Thee, yea, to Thee,
To Thee, true, to Thee,
To Thee, Lord, is the sover-
eignty:
To Him is it becoming,
To Him shall it become!'

זַכַּאי בִּמְלוּכָה · חָסִין
כַּהֲלָכָה · טַפְסְרָיו יֹאמְרוּ לוֹ ·
לְךָ וּלְךָ · לְךָ כִּי לְךָ · לְךָ אַף
לְךָ · לְךָ יְיָ הַמַּמְלָכָה · כִּי לוֹ
נָאֶה · כִּי לוֹ יָאֶה:

Single in kingship, Mighty of
right!
To Him say His wise ones:
'To Thee, and to Thee,
To Thee, yea, to Thee,
To Thee, true, to Thee,
To Thee, Lord, is the sover-
eignty:
To Him is it becoming,
To Him shall it become!'

יָחִיד בִּמְלוּכָה · כַּבִּיר
כַּהֲלָכָה · לִמּוּדָיו יֹאמְרוּ לוֹ ·
לְךָ וּלְךָ · לְךָ כִּי לְךָ · לְךָ אַף
לְךָ · לְךָ יְיָ הַמַּמְלָכָה · כִּי לוֹ
נָאֶה · כִּי לוֹ יָאֶה:

Exalted in kingship, Reverèd
of right!
To Him say those around
Him:
'To Thee, and to Thee,
To Thee, yea, to Thee,
To Thee, true, to Thee,
To Thee, Lord, is the sover-
eignty:
To Him is it becoming,
To Him shall it become!'

מָרוֹם בִּמְלוּכָה · נוֹרָא
כַּהֲלָכָה · סְבִיבָיו יֹאמְרוּ לוֹ ·
לְךָ וּלְךָ · לְךָ כִּי לְךָ · לְךָ אַף
לְךָ · לְךָ יְיָ הַמַּמְלָכָה · כִּי לוֹ
נָאֶה · כִּי לוֹ יָאֶה:

Gentle in kingship, Redeem-
ing of right!
To Him say His righteous:
'To Thee, and to Thee,

עָנָיו בִּמְלוּכָה · פּוֹדֶה
כַּהֲלָכָה · צַדִּיקָיו יֹאמְרוּ לוֹ ·

To Thee, yea, to Thee,
To Thee, true, to Thee,
To Thee, Lord, is the sover-
eignty:
To Him is it becoming,
To Him shall it become!'

לְךָ וּלְךָ · לְךָ כִּי לְךָ · לְךָ אַף
לְךָ · לְךָ יְיָ הַמַּמְלָכָה · כִּי לוֹ
נָאֶה · כִּי לוֹ יָאֶה:

Holy in kingship, Merciful
of right!
To Him say His myriads:
'To Thee, and to Thee,
To Thee, yea, to Thee,
To Thee, true, to Thee,
To Thee, Lord, is the sover-
eignty:
To Him is it becoming,
To Him shall it become!'

קָדוֹשׁ בִּמְלוּכָה · רַחוּם
כַּהֲלָכָה · שִׁנְאַנָּיו יֹאמְרוּ לוֹ ·
לְךָ וּלְךָ · לְךָ כִּי לְךָ · לְךָ אַף
לְךָ · לְךָ יְיָ הַמַּמְלָכָה · כִּי לוֹ
נָאֶה · כִּי לוֹ יָאֶה:

Excellent in kingship, Sus-
taining of right!
To Him say His perfect:
'To Thee, and to Thee,
To Thee, yea, to Thee,
To Thee, true, to Thee,
To Thee, Lord, is the sover-
eignty:
To Him is it becoming,
To Him shall it become!'

תַּקִּיף בִּמְלוּכָה · תּוֹמֵךְ
כַּהֲלָכָה · תְּמִימָיו יֹאמְרוּ לוֹ ·
לְךָ וּלְךָ · לְךָ כִּי לְךָ · לְךָ אַף
לְךָ · לְךָ יְיָ הַמַּמְלָכָה · כִּי לוֹ
נָאֶה · כִּי לוֹ יָאֶה:

77

STRONG IS HE!
May He build His temple
speedily!
Rapidly, rapidly, In our days
speedily!
God, O, build, God, O, build,
Build Thy temple speedily!

אַדִּיר הוּא · יִבְנֶה בֵיתוֹ
בְּקָרוֹב · בִּמְהֵרָה · בִּמְהֵרָה ·
בְּיָמֵינוּ בְּקָרוֹב · אֵל בְּנֵה · אֵל
בְּנֵה · בְּנֵה בֵיתְךָ בְּקָרוֹב:

Choice is He, Great is He,
Foremost He!
May He build His temple
speedily!
Rapidly, rapidly, In our days
speedily!
God, O, build, God, O, build,
Build Thy temple speedily!

בָּחוּר הוּא · גָּדוֹל הוּא ·
דָּגוּל הוּא · יִבְנֶה בֵיתוֹ בְּקָרוֹב ·
בִּמְהֵרָה · בִּמְהֵרָה · בְּיָמֵינוּ
בְּקָרוֹב · אֵל בְּנֵה · אֵל בְּנֵה ·
בְּנֵה בֵיתְךָ בְּקָרוֹב:

Glorious He, Trusty He,
Guileless He!
May He build His temple
speedily!
Rapidly, rapidly, In our days
speedily!
God, O, build, God, O, build,
Build Thy temple speedily!

הָדוּר הוּא · וָתִיק הוּא · זַכַּאי
הוּא · יִבְנֶה בֵיתוֹ בְּקָרוֹב ·
בִּמְהֵרָה · בִּמְהֵרָה · בְּיָמֵינוּ
בְּקָרוֹב · אֵל בְּנֵה · אֵל בְּנֵה ·
בְּנֵה בֵיתְךָ בְּקָרוֹב:

Righteous He, Pure is He,
One is He!
May He build His temple
speedily!
Rapidly, rapidly, In our days
speedily!
God, O, build, God, O, build,
Build Thy temple speedily!

חָסִיד הוּא · טָהוֹר הוּא ·
יָחִיד הוּא · יִבְנֶה בֵיתוֹ בְּקָרוֹב ·
בִּמְהֵרָה · בִּמְהֵרָה · בְּיָמֵינוּ
בְּקָרוֹב · אֵל בְּנֵה · אֵל בְּנֵה ·
בְּנֵה בֵיתְךָ בְּקָרוֹב:

78

Mighty He, Wise is He,
King is He!
May He build His temple
speedily!
Rapidly, rapidly, In our days
speedily!
God, O, build, God, O, build,
Build Thy temple speedily!

כַּבִּיר הוּא · לָמוּד הוּא ·
מֶלֶךְ הוּא · יִבְנֶה בֵיתוֹ
בְּקָרוֹב · בִּמְהֵרָה · בִּמְהֵרָה ·
בְּיָמֵינוּ בְּקָרוֹב · אֵל בְּנֵה · אֵל
בְּנֵה · בְּנֵה בֵיתְךָ בְּקָרוֹב:

Tremendous He, Exalted
He, Powerful He!
May He build His temple
speedily!
Rapidly, rapidly, In our days
speedily!
God, O, build, God, O, build,
Build Thy temple speedily!

נָאוֹר הוּא · סַגִּיב הוּא ·
עִזּוּז הוּא · יִבְנֶה בֵיתוֹ
בְּקָרוֹב · בִּמְהֵרָה · בִּמְהֵרָה ·
בְּיָמֵינוּ בְּקָרוֹב · אֵל בְּנֵה · אֵל
בְּנֵה · בְּנֵה בֵיתְךָ בְּקָרוֹב:

Redeeming He, Good is He,
Holy He!
May He build His temple
speedily!
Rapidly, rapidly, In our days
speedily!
God, O, build, God, O, build,
Build Thy temple speedily!

פּוֹדֶה הוּא · צַדִּיק הוּא ·
קָדוֹשׁ הוּא · יִבְנֶה בֵיתוֹ
בְּקָרוֹב · בִּמְהֵרָה · בִּמְהֵרָה ·
בְּיָמֵינוּ בְּקָרוֹב · אֵל בְּנֵה · אֵל
בְּנֵה · בְּנֵה בֵיתְךָ בְּקָרוֹב:

Merciful He, Almighty He,
Lord is He!
May He build His temple
speedily!
Rapidly, rapidly, In our days
speedily!
God, O, build, God, O, build,
Build Thy temple speedily!

רַחוּם הוּא · שַׁדַּי הוּא ·
תַּקִּיף הוּא · יִבְנֶה בֵיתוֹ
בְּקָרוֹב · בִּמְהֵרָה · בִּמְהֵרָה ·
בְּיָמֵינוּ בְּקָרוֹב · אֵל בְּנֵה · אֵל
בְּנֵה · בְּנֵה בֵיתְךָ בְּקָרוֹב:

79

Who knows one? One I know!

One is our God in Heaven and on Earth.

אֶחָד מִי יוֹדֵעַ · אֶחָד אֲנִי
יוֹדֵעַ · אֶחָד אֱלֹהֵינוּ שֶׁבַּשָּׁמַיִם
וּבָאָרֶץ:

Who knows Two? Two I know!

Two are the Tables of Covenant:

One is our God in Heaven and on Earth.

שְׁנַיִם מִי יוֹדֵעַ · שְׁנַיִם אֲנִי
יוֹדֵעַ · שְׁנֵי לֻחוֹת הַבְּרִית ·
אֶחָד אֱלֹהֵינוּ שֶׁבַּשָּׁמַיִם
וּבָאָרֶץ:

Who knows Three? Three I know!

Three are the Fathers:
Two the Tables of Covenant:
One is our God in Heaven and on Earth.

שְׁלֹשָׁה מִי יוֹדֵעַ · שְׁלֹשָׁה
אֲנִי יוֹדֵעַ · שְׁלֹשָׁה אָבוֹת · שְׁנֵי
לֻחוֹת הַבְּרִית · אֶחָד אֱלֹהֵינוּ
שֶׁבַּשָּׁמַיִם וּבָאָרֶץ:

Who knows Four? Four I know!

Four are the Mothers:
Three are the Fathers:
Two the Tables of Covenant:

אַרְבַּע מִי יוֹדֵעַ · אַרְבַּע אֲנִי
יוֹדֵעַ · אַרְבַּע אִמָּהוֹת · שְׁלֹשָׁה
אָבוֹת · שְׁנֵי לֻחוֹת הַבְּרִית ·

WHO KNOWS ONE? The hymns which conclude the *Haggadah* have progressively become more and more popular in character. 'Who knows one?' is a typical mediæval 'madrigal of numbers'. The fashion is possibly Eastern in origin, like so many others; but the practice is, as a matter of fact, by no means an unnatural one, and is quite likely to have developed spontaneously in more than one age or country, without any necessary interaction. In mediæval Germany there was a peasant drinking-song of this sort, which was adapted by the monks to religious purposes. This may conceivably have been the origin of the present poem. To the Jew, however, the dividing line between everyday life and religion did not exist: and it is difficult to say whether the Hebrew version is in origin a song or a hymn. There are parallels in Greek, in Old German, and in half the languages of modern Europe. To English readers, 'Green grow the rushes, O' and 'We will all gae sing, boys', provide a close and familiar parallel.

There is, however, one striking difference between the Hebrew and the vernacular versions. To the Christian, thirteen was an unlucky number: and the European parallels stop, therefore, when they reach twelve. To the Jew, however, this superstition had no appeal: and perhaps he even made a point of neglecting it. Moreover, to him thirteen had a certain mystical value, being the numerical equivalent of the word *Ehad* (One), symbolizing the unity of God: and he therefore felt all the more impelled to continue till he reached that number.

C

One is our God in Heaven
and on Earth.

אֶחָד אֱלֹהֵינוּ שֶׁבַּשָּׁמַיִם
וּבָאָרֶץ:

Who knows Five? Five I
know!
Five are the Books of the
Law:
Four are the Mothers:
Three are the Fathers:
Two the Tables of Covenant:
One is our God in Heaven
and on Earth.

חֲמִשָּׁה מִי יוֹדֵעַ · חֲמִשָּׁה
אֲנִי יוֹדֵעַ · חֲמִשָּׁה חֻמְשֵׁי
תוֹרָה · אַרְבַּע אִמָּהוֹת · שְׁלֹשָׁה
אָבוֹת · שְׁנֵי לֻחוֹת הַבְּרִית ·
אֶחָד אֱלֹהֵינוּ שֶׁבַּשָּׁמַיִם
וּבָאָרֶץ:

Who knows Six? Six I know!
Six are the Orders of the
Mishnah:
Five the Books of the Law:
Four are the Mothers:
Three are the Fathers:
Two the Tables of Covenant:
One is our God in Heaven
and on Earth.

שִׁשָּׁה מִי יוֹדֵעַ · שִׁשָּׁה אֲנִי
יוֹדֵעַ · שִׁשָּׁה סִדְרֵי מִשְׁנָה ·
חֲמִשָּׁה חֻמְשֵׁי תוֹרָה · אַרְבַּע
אִמָּהוֹת · שְׁלֹשָׁה אָבוֹת · שְׁנֵי
לֻחוֹת הַבְּרִית · אֶחָד אֱלֹהֵינוּ
שֶׁבַּשָּׁמַיִם וּבָאָרֶץ:

Who knows Seven? Seven I
know!
Seven are the days of the
Week:
Six are the Orders of the
Mishnah:
Five the Books of the Law:
Four are the Mothers:
Three are the Fathers:
Two the Tables of Covenant:
One is our God in Heaven
and on Earth.

שִׁבְעָה מִי יוֹדֵעַ · שִׁבְעָה אֲנִי
יוֹדֵעַ · שִׁבְעָה יְמֵי שַׁבַּתָּא ·
שִׁשָּׁה סִדְרֵי מִשְׁנָה · חֲמִשָּׁה
חֻמְשֵׁי תוֹרָה · אַרְבַּע אִמָּהוֹת ·
שְׁלֹשָׁה אָבוֹת · שְׁנֵי לֻחוֹת
הַבְּרִית · אֶחָד אֱלֹהֵינוּ
שֶׁבַּשָּׁמַיִם וּבָאָרֶץ:

81

Who knows Eight? Eight I
know!
Eight are the days of the
Covenant:
Seven are the days of the
Week:
Six are the Orders of the
Mishnah:
Five the Books of the Law:
Four are the Mothers:
Three are the Fathers:
Two the Tables of Covenant:
One is our God in Heaven
and on Earth.

שְׁמוֹנָה מִי יוֹדֵעַ · שְׁמוֹנָה
אֲנִי יוֹדֵעַ · שְׁמוֹנָה יְמֵי מִילָה ·
שִׁבְעָה יְמֵי שַׁבַּתָּא · שִׁשָּׁה
סִדְרֵי מִשְׁנָה · חֲמִשָּׁה חֻמְשֵׁי
תוֹרָה · אַרְבַּע אִמָּהוֹת · שְׁלֹשָׁה
אָבוֹת · שְׁנֵי לֻחוֹת הַבְּרִית ·
אֶחָד אֱלֹהֵינוּ שֶׁבַּשָּׁמַיִם
וּבָאָרֶץ:

Who knows Nine? Nine I
know!
Nine are the months of
Carrying:
Eight are the days of the
Covenant:
Seven are the days of the
Week:
Six are the Orders of the
Mishnah:
Five the Books of the Law:
Four are the Mothers:
Three are the Fathers:
Two the Tables of Covenant:
One is our God in Heaven
and on Earth.

תִּשְׁעָה מִי יוֹדֵעַ · תִּשְׁעָה
אֲנִי יוֹדֵעַ · תִּשְׁעָה יַרְחֵי לֵדָה ·
שְׁמוֹנָה יְמֵי מִילָה · שִׁבְעָה יְמֵי
שַׁבַּתָּא · שִׁשָּׁה סִדְרֵי מִשְׁנָה ·
חֲמִשָּׁה חֻמְשֵׁי תוֹרָה · אַרְבַּע
אִמָּהוֹת · שְׁלֹשָׁה אָבוֹת · שְׁנֵי
לֻחוֹת הַבְּרִית · אֶחָד אֱלֹהֵינוּ
שֶׁבַּשָּׁמַיִם וּבָאָרֶץ:

Who knows Ten? Ten I
know!
Ten are the Commandments:
Nine are the months of
Carrying:
Eight are the days of the
Covenant:
Seven, the days of the Week:
Six are the Orders of the
Mishnah:
Five the Books of the Law:
Four are the Mothers:
Three are the Fathers:
Two the Tables of Covenant:
One is our God in Heaven
and on Earth.

עֲשָׂרָה מִי יוֹדֵעַ. עֲשָׂרָה
אֲנִי יוֹדֵעַ. עֲשָׂרָה דִבְּרַיָּא.
תִּשְׁעָה יַרְחֵי לֵדָה. שְׁמוֹנָה
יְמֵי מִילָה. שִׁבְעָה יְמֵי שַׁבַּתָּא.
שִׁשָּׁה סִדְרֵי מִשְׁנָה. חֲמִשָּׁה
חֻמְשֵׁי תוֹרָה. אַרְבַּע אִמָּהוֹת.
שְׁלֹשָׁה אָבוֹת. שְׁנֵי לֻחוֹת
הַבְּרִית. אֶחָד אֱלֹהֵינוּ
שֶׁבַּשָּׁמַיִם וּבָאָרֶץ:

Who knows Eleven? Eleven
I know!
Eleven are the Stars:
Ten are the Commandments:
Nine are the months of
Carrying:
Eight are the days of the
Covenant:
Seven, the days of the Week:
Six are the Orders of the
Mishnah:
Five the Books of the Law:
Four are the Mothers:
Three are the Fathers:
Two the Tables of Covenant:
One is our God in Heaven
and on Earth.

אַחַד עָשָׂר מִי יוֹדֵעַ. אַחַד
עָשָׂר אֲנִי יוֹדֵעַ. אַחַד עָשָׂר
כּוֹכְבַיָּא. עֲשָׂרָה דִבְּרַיָּא.
תִּשְׁעָה יַרְחֵי לֵדָה. שְׁמוֹנָה
יְמֵי מִילָה. שִׁבְעָה יְמֵי שַׁבַּתָּא.
שִׁשָּׁה סִדְרֵי מִשְׁנָה. חֲמִשָּׁה
חֻמְשֵׁי תוֹרָה. אַרְבַּע אִמָּהוֹת.
שְׁלֹשָׁה אָבוֹת. שְׁנֵי לֻחוֹת
הַבְּרִית. אֶחָד אֱלֹהֵינוּ
שֶׁבַּשָּׁמַיִם וּבָאָרֶץ:

Who knows Twelve? Twelve
I know!

Twelve are the Tribes:
Eleven are the Stars:
Ten are the Commandments:
Nine are the months of
Carrying:
Eight are the days of the
Covenant:
Seven are the days of the
Week:
Six are the Orders of the
Mishnah:
Five the Books of the Law:
Four are the Mothers:
Three are the Fathers:
Two the Tables of Covenant:
One is our God in Heaven
and on Earth.

שְׁנֵים עָשָׂר מִי יוֹדֵעַ. שְׁנֵים
עָשָׂר אֲנִי יוֹדֵעַ. שְׁנֵים עָשָׂר
שִׁבְטַיָּא. אַחַד עָשָׂר כּוֹכְבַיָּא.
עֲשָׂרָה דִבְּרַיָּא. תִּשְׁעָה יַרְחֵי
לֵדָה. שְׁמוֹנָה יְמֵי מִילָה.
שִׁבְעָה יְמֵי שַׁבַּתָּא. שִׁשָּׁה
סִדְרֵי מִשְׁנָה. חֲמִשָּׁה חֻמְשֵׁי
תוֹרָה. אַרְבַּע אִמָּהוֹת. שְׁלשָׁה
אָבוֹת. שְׁנֵי לֻחוֹת הַבְּרִית.
אֶחָד אֱלֹהֵינוּ שֶׁבַּשָׁמַיִם
וּבָאָרֶץ:

Who knows Thirteen? Thir-
teen I know!

Thirteen are the Attributes
of God:
Twelve are the Tribes:
Eleven are the Stars:
Ten are the Commandments:
Nine are the months of
Carrying:
Eight are the days of the
Covenant:
Seven are the days of the
Week:
Six are the Orders of the
Mishnah:

שְׁלשָׁה עָשָׂר מִי יוֹדֵעַ.
שְׁלשָׁה עָשָׂר אֲנִי יוֹדֵעַ.
שְׁלשָׁה עָשָׂר מִדַּיָּא. שְׁנֵים
עָשָׂר שִׁבְטַיָּא. אַחַד עָשָׂר
כּוֹכְבַיָּא. עֲשָׂרָה דִבְּרַיָּא.
תִּשְׁעָה יַרְחֵי לֵדָה. שְׁמוֹנָה יְמֵי
מִילָה. שִׁבְעָה יְמֵי שַׁבַּתָּא.
שִׁשָּׁה סִדְרֵי מִשְׁנָה. חֲמִשָּׁה

Five the Books of the Law:	חֲמִשֵׁי תוֹרָה · אַרְבַּע אִמָּהוֹת ·
Four are the Mothers:	
Three are the Fathers:	שְׁלֹשָׁה אָבוֹת · שְׁנֵי לֻחוֹת
Two the Tables of Covenant:	
One is our God in Heaven	הַבְּרִית · אֶחָד אֱלֹהֵינוּ
and on Earth.	
	שֶׁבַּשָּׁמַיִם וּבָאָרֶץ :

ONE ONLY KID

Of all the hymns recited at the close of the *Haggadah*, none is more curious and none more popular than the *Had Gadya*. It is, in fact, little removed from a nursery-rhyme. The familiar 'House that Jack Built', in English, is based upon the same principle; but the identical type exists also in German, French, Portuguese, Greek, and even Siamese. There are few specimens of the ubiquitous nursery-rhyme which are more widely spread

The question remains, Which is the original, the Jewish form or the secular? Whole volumes have been written to decide the problem. Some pundits assert that the *Had Gadya* is based upon the famous Old German nursery-rhyme, *Der Herr der schickt den Jokel aus*, which was generally sung upon the feast of St. Lambert (September 17th): itself, as a matter of fact, probably the imitation of an older French original. This theory is by no means surely established. The language in which the song is written — Aramaic, not pure Hebrew — would point to a fairly early origin: certainly anterior to the fifteenth century, when the upholders of the Germanic theory would date it. Nor can the fact that it is to be found only in the Ashkenazic ritual for the Seder be adduced in support of its German origin: for the song early became popular in France and Italy, and is to be found in secular usage even among the Sephardim of the Orient. Indeed, it would not be difficult to construct a plausible argument to prove that the literary influence has been in the reverse direction, from the Hebrew to the modern European languages: for the *Had Gadya* has always been a favourite subject for translation, and is found in vernacular versions of considerable antiquity in Spanish, French, and Provençal. The truth of the matter lies, in all probability, midway between the two- extremes. Both the Hebrew and the European songs most likely follow some ancient prototype, perhaps Oriental, which is common to both. It is, indeed, a very natural style of children's rhyme, which may well have grown up independently amongst different peoples without any need for imitation, conscious or unconscious.

This does not, however, solve the more difficult, and perhaps more important, problem: that of the inclusion of this song in the *Haggadah*, under any circumstances, whether it be original or imitative. After all, it is childish in conception and absolutely secular in subject: and it would seem to be eminently out of place in what is, finally speaking, a religious service. But the Seder is above all a ritual for the children. It is for them that these songs at the end were especially intended. Nothing could be more certain of riveting their attention or of assisting them to defy the growing bonds of slumber than these. This was especially the case with this, the last and most delightful of all: and the Rabbis assuredly showed themselves, once more, shrewd psychologists in including it.

Nor was it impossible to give a reasonable justification. The *Had Gadya* is not quite so simple as it looks. Written in the form of a nursery-rhyme, phrased in the most elementary language, it nevertheless inculcates from beginning to end a lesson of permanent value, which no child can be too young to learn. It shows us, in the simplest terms, how every creature is responsible for

ONE ONLY KID,
One only kid,
That father bought for two
zuzim,
One only kid, One only kid.

חַד גַּדְיָא חַד גַּדְיָא דְּזַבֵּן
אַבָּא בִּתְרֵי זוּזֵי.
חַד גַּדְיָא חַד גַּדְיָא:

Then came a cat
And ate the kid
That father bought for two
zuzim,
One only kid, One only kid.

וְאָתָא שׁוּנְרָא. וְאָכְלָה
לְגַדְיָא. דְּזַבֵּן אַבָּא בִּתְרֵי זוּזֵי.
חַד גַּדְיָא חַד גַּדְיָא:

its actions, how every being knows some power higher than itself, and how, finally, above all, there exists a Supreme Being, capable of conquering even death, from whose judgement there is no appeal. Perhaps the tale of the beating of the dog which bit the cat which ate the kid is as useful a lesson as any exposition of dogmatic theology: while the position at the head of the list of the Holy One, Blessed be He, beyond whom there is nothing further, summarises with admirable conciseness the Jewish attitude to life.

So simple an explanation, however, has not generally been considered sufficient. The prominent position of this folk-song in the Jewish liturgy has led to the belief that there must necessarily be some significance, deeper and more profound, underlying it. Accordingly, a whole literature has grown up round the little poem. This does not consist merely of works (like those of Henry George, in English, and of Arthur Carlos de Barros Basto in Portuguese) endeavouring to show that here is to be sought the original of certain poems familiar in the folk-lore of their respective countries. It includes also profound monographs, fortified by all the panoply of scientific apparatus, in which an attempt is made to prove that behind these rhymes there lies a mystical or philosophic meaning, and that with all its seemingly simple form the little poem enshrines the key to the great truths of human existence. Many Jewish scholars of the old school compiled treatises on the subject — men like Moses ben Jacob Aberle, Asher Anshel,

86

Then came a dog
And bit the cat
That ate the kid
That father bought for two
zuzim,
One only kid, One only kid.

וְאָתָא כַלְבָּא · וְנָשַׁךְ
לְשׁוּנְרָא · דְּאָכְלָה לְגַּדְיָא ·
דְּזַבִּן אַבָּא בִּתְרֵי זוּזֵי ·
חַד גַּדְיָא חַד גַּדְיָא:

Then came a stick
And beat the dog
That bit the cat
That ate the kid
That father bought for two
zuzim,
One only kid, One only kid.

וְאָתָא חוּטְרָא · וְהִכָּה
לְכַלְבָּא · דְּנָשַׁךְ לְשׁוּנְרָא ·
דְּאָכְלָה לְגַּדְיָא · דְּזַבִּן אַבָּא
בִּתְרֵי זוּזֵי ·
חַד גַּדְיָא חַד גַּדְיָא:

Moses Blumenfeld, Judah Judel, and even Jonathan Eybeschütz, to mention only a few. What is more surprising, several Christian students like Philip Lebrecht and Herbert von der Hardt thought it worth their while to devote their energies to its elucidation. Wagenseil thought that it referred to the Fall of man and his Redemption. Christian Andreas Teuber regarded it as a parable of God's providence in the human race.

To seek so recondite a meaning in so very simple a rhyme is perhaps too much. Nevertheless, the tale may well be taken — as has now become usual — as symbolical of the course of Jewish history. The Kid, according to this reading, stands for Israel: acquired as a perpetual possession by his heavenly Father with the two tables of stone which contained the Law (or, according to another explanation, through His two emissaries, Moses and Aaron). The Cat represents Assyria, the conqueror of Israel; the Dog, Babylon, which succeeded Assyria: the Stick, Persia, through whom the Babylonian power fell; the Water, Greece, which engulfed Persia; the Ox, Rome,

Then came the fire
And burned the stick
That beat the dog
That bit the cat
That ate the kid
That father bought for two
zuzim,
One only kid, One only kid.

וְאָתָא נוּרָא · וְשָׂרַף לְחוּטְרָא ·
דְּהִכָּה לְכַלְבָּא · דְּנָשַׁךְ
לְשׁוּנְרָא · דְּאָכְלָה לְגַדְיָא ·
דְּזַבִּן אַבָּא בִּתְרֵי זוּזֵי ·
חַד גַּדְיָא חַד גַּדְיָא :

Then water came
And quenched the fire
That burned the stick
That beat the dog
That bit the cat
That ate the kid
That father bought for two
zuzim,
One only kid, One only kid.

וְאָתָא מַיָּא · וְכָבָה לְנוּרָא ·
דְּשָׂרַף לְחוּטְרָא · דְּהִכָּה
לְכַלְבָּא · דְּנָשַׁךְ לְשׁוּנְרָא ·
דְּאָכְלָה לְגַדְיָא · דְּזַבִּן אַבָּא
בִּתְרֵי זוּזֵי ·
חַד גַּדְיָא חַד גַּדְיָא :

which conquered Greece; the Slaughterer, the Moslems, who finally broke the power of Rome; the Angel of Death, the European nations, who succeeded to the Moslems. But in the end the Holy One, Blessed be He, will assuredly come to re-establish the principle of justice on the earth and to redeem His children from the oppressor. The *Haggadah* can end upon no more fitting note.

Then came an ox
And drank the water
That quenched the fire
That burned the stick
That beat the dog
That bit the cat
That ate the kid
That father bought for two
    zuzim,
One only kid, One only kid.

וְאָתָא תוֹרָא · וְשָׁתָא לְמַיָּא ·
דְּכָבָה לְנוּרָא · דְּשָׂרַף
לְחוּטְרָא · דְּהִכָּה לְכַלְבָּא ·
דְּנָשַׁךְ לְשׁוּנְרָא · דְּאָכְלָה
לְגַדְיָא · דְּזַבֵּן אַבָּא בִּתְרֵי זוּזֵי ·
חַד גַּדְיָא חַד גַּדְיָא :

Then came the slaughterer
And slaughtered the ox
That drank the water
That quenched the fire
That burned the stick
That beat the dog
That bit the cat
That ate the kid
That father bought for two
    zuzim,
One only kid, One only kid.

וְאָתָא שׁוֹחֵט · וְשָׁחַט לְתוֹרָא ·
דְּשָׁתָא לְמַיָּא · דְּכָבָה לְנוּרָא ·
דְּשָׂרַף לְחוּטְרָא · דְּהִכָּה
לְכַלְבָּא · דְּנָשַׁךְ לְשׁוּנְרָא ·
דְּאָכְלָה לְגַדְיָא · דְּזַבֵּן אַבָּא
בִּתְרֵי זוּזֵי ·
חַד גַּדְיָא חַד גַּדְיָא :

Then came the Angel of
    Death
And slew the slaughterer
That slaughtered the ox
That drank the water
That quenched the fire
That burned the stick
That beat the dog
That bit the cat
That ate the kid
That father bought for two
    zuzim,
One only kid, One only kid.

וְאָתָא מַלְאַךְ הַמָּוֶת · וְשָׁחַט
לְשׁוֹחֵט · דְּשָׁחַט לְתוֹרָא ·
דְּשָׁתָא לְמַיָּא · דְּכָבָה לְנוּרָא ·
דְּשָׂרַף לְחוּטְרָא · דְּהִכָּה
לְכַלְבָּא · דְּנָשַׁךְ לְשׁוּנְרָא ·
דְּאָכְלָה לְגַדְיָא · דְּזַבֵּן אַבָּא
בִּתְרֵי זוּזֵי ·
חַד גַּדְיָא חַד גַּדְיָא :

Then came the Holy One,
    Blessed be He
And smote the Angel of
    Death
That slew the slaughterer
That slaughtered the ox
That drank the water
That quenched the fire
That burned the stick

וְאָתָא הַקָּדוֹשׁ בָּרוּךְ הוּא ·
וְשָׁחַט לְמַלְאַךְ הַמָּוֶת · דְּשָׁחַט
לְשׁוֹחֵט · דְּשָׁחַט לְתוֹרָא ·
דְּשָׁתָא לְמַיָּא · דְּכָבָה לְנוּרָא ·
דְּשָׂרַף לְחוּטְרָא · דְּהִכָּה

That beat the dog
That bit the cat
That ate the kid
That father bought for two
    zuzim,
One only kid, One only kid.

לְכַלְבָּא · דְּנָשַׁךְ לְשׁוּנְרָא ·
דְּאָכְלָה לְגַדְיָא · דְּזַבַּן אַבָּא
בִּתְרֵי זוּזֵי ·
חַד גַּדְיָא חַד גַּדְיָא:

FINIS